Smart Crockery Cooking

Over 100 Delicious Recipes

Carol Heding Munson

Sterling Publishing Co., Inc.   New York

Library of Congress Cataloging-in-Publication Data

Munson, Carol.
   Smart crockery cooking : over 100 delicious recipes / by Carol
Heding Munson.
      p.   cm.
   Includes index.
   ISBN 0-8069-6106-6
   1. Electric cookery, Slow. 2. Casserole cookery. I. Title.
TX827.M86 1996
641.5'884–dc20   96–26158
                                                                                    CIP

10 9 8 7 6

Published by Sterling Publishing Company, Inc.
387 Park Avenue South, New York, N.Y. 10016
© 1996 by Carol Heding Munson
Distributed in Canada by Sterling Publishing
   %Canadian Manda Group, One Atlantic Avenue, Suite 105
   Toronto, Ontario, Canada M6K 3E7
Distributed in Great Britain and Europe by Cassell PLC
   Wellington House, 125 Strand, London WC2R 0BB, England
Distributed in Australia by Capricorn Link (Australia) Pty Ltd.
   P.O. Box 6651, Baulkham Hills, Business Centre,
   NSW 2153, Australia
Manufactured in the United States of America
All rights reserved

Sterling ISBN 0-8069-6106-6

Contents

Introduction

My situation is hardly unique: At the end of an 8- to 9-hour business day I'm bushed, and the family's hungry. Even as I write this, I can hear the clamors: "What's for dinner? When do we eat?" Then comes the surprise: "Got to be at practice in 30 minutes." And so, from a need for instant meals, a rewarding reliance on the slow cooker began.

Early in the day, when I feel fresh, I can toss a few ingredients into the slow cooker, then let it do its thing: simmer up a robust stew, or a light soup, or a flavorful pasta sauce. In the evening, when I'm ready to eat, dinner's done.

As my success with this versatile cooker grew, I wanted to share my best experiences with other cooking enthusiasts. What followed is this book, which is packed with fast-to-fix entrees, side dishes, and desserts. These recipes are good for you—meaning low in fat and low in sodium. What's more, each has a marvelous marriage of flavors that comes only from lengthy cooking.

From the international favorites to the home-style dishes, every recipe that appears here had pass muster not only with adults who enjoy gourmet foods, but with my teenagers—independent critics with sharp taste buds and uninhibited opinions. Only the tastiest recipes survived.

Do hurry to start slow cooking some quick, healthy meals. Feel free to experiment with variations—who knows, you may even create enough favorite new combinations to fill your own cookbook. Along the way, though, you'll experience another reward of slow cooking: the sensory pleasure of coming home to mouthwatering aromas. Dinner's ready!

Acknowledgments
A hearty thank you to Russell and Roger, who critiqued every recipe and enthusiastically offered opinions. And a loving thank you to Lowell for his invaluable assistance and encouragement with recipe and manuscript development and his cheerful handling of the daily supermarket shuttle.

Slow & Easy Cooking Basics

Quick, quick! For tantalizing aromas and intense flavors in meals that virtually cook themselves, get out your slow cooker. Read the pages that follow; they're jam-packed with hints and tips for getting the most from this special, time-saving appliance. It's truly a busy cook's best friend.

ABOUT SLOW COOKERS

Logical it isn't, practical it is: Slow cooking makes for fast, great-tasting meals that suit your schedule. Here's how the process works: Early in the day, ingredients are prepared and go into an electric slow cooker, where they simmer and blend for three to eight unattended hours. Then, whenever you say, "Let's eat," a fabulous main event—entrée, stew, or soup—is ready for serving.

The concept of slow cooking has been around for centuries. Electric slow cookers became hot items in the early 1970s, but a decade or so later, many cooks considered them unsophisticated relics of a bygone era. Not so, say the slow-cooker manufacturers. According to them, the handy appliances never really went out of style; millions of cooks (including me) continued to buy and use them for their intrinsic benefits. Now they're making a fashion comeback, and for good reasons!

WHY WAIT?

The slow cooker, sometimes called the crockery pot, is very energy efficient. When set to LOW, it actually draws less electricity than a 100-watt light bulb. The cooker, therefore, is economical to use and won't overheat the kitchen, even when simmering a roast for 10 to 12 hours. It also fits nicely on any countertop and stores handily in pantries as well.

More reasons to take it slow: Gentle all-day simmering tenderizes lean meats and sturdy vegetables (carrots, rutabagas, potatoes, winter squash) for high-flavor, low-fat meals. And low cooking temperatures—200°F (93.3°C) when set on LOW; 300°F (149°C) on HIGH—mean that timing is flexible. A half-hour more or less won't spoil your meal.

Still more advantages: Most slow cooker recipes can be put together in 15 to 30 minutes. The cook need only measure and chop the ingredients, toss everything into the pot, and turn it on. (Some recipes also suggest sautéing meat, onions, or other ingredients before cooking for added flavor.) Several hours later, depending on the heat setting selected and the fullness of the pot, dinner's done. Could meal preparation get any easier or quicker? Well, perhaps, two meals for the work of one. Now, we're cooking! Depending on the size of the pot, slow cookers can handle food for a small crowd, so you can easily double small recipes or select ones that make 8 or 10 servings.

COOKER STYLES

Slow cookers come in two basic shapes—round and rectangular—and in standard sizes that range from 3 to 6 quarts. Less common are mini 1- and 2-quart cookers. Most of the minis, which may be battery operated, are electric and are designed to work on standard household current. Cords are short, so units must be placed near outlets.

At the core of most round slow cookers is a heavy ceramic bowl, which may or may not be removable. The bowl is surrounded by a metal sheaf that encases electric heating coils. Rectangular cookers have a removable nonstick metal bowl (really more like a high-sided pan) that sits on a multi-purpose base, which encloses a heating element with a temperature selection dial. Depending on the model and price, both types can be bought with either snug-fitting glass or lightweight plastic lids. The plastic lids stay somewhat cooler to the touch, but may turn opaque if you use your cooker a lot.

Buying a new slow cooker? Check out seasonal sales at major chain stores for price discounts up to 50%. Be sure to get one with a removable bowl even if the whole thing costs a bit more. It's worth the few extra dollars. Why? You can submerge the bowl in water for easy washing. And you can stash it in the refrigerator if you've prepared ingredients beforehand. When you're ready to cook, simply return the bowl to the unit and turn the switch on. Both ceramic and metal bowls are oven-safe, although ceramic ones aren't broiler-safe and metal ones can't go in a microwave. Ceramic bowls aren't for stove-top use, either; any sautéing before cooking must be done in a skillet—a minor inconvenience.

The beauty of a slow cooker is its plug-and-cook feature: toss everything in the pot, switch it on, and let the pot do its cooking thing. But can it really go the distance unattended? Yes, for the most part.

Experience indicates that some foods, such as pot roasts that cook for 10 hours, will occasionally stick in cookers that have bottom-only heating elements. An infrequent stir–once every two hours or so–takes care of the problem.

For even cooking, dishes that require *very* little liquid can benefit from a stir as well. About halfway through cooking, stir to reverse the ingredients on the top and those on the bottom. Enjoy experimenting with your cooker; recipes react differently to each one, depending on things like bowl size, type of cooker, heat setting, and food density.

When it comes to cooking times, expect differences. All slow cookers are not necessarily equal. The accuracy of a cooker's thermostat and the location of heating elements (surrounding a ceramic bowl or below a metal one) can speed or slow cooking by a couple of hours. Is one better than another? It's difficult to say, since other factors also come into play: voltage fluctuations, how cold food is at the start of cooking, how often the lid is picked up, how full the pot is, and the density of ingredients. No matter which cooker you select–or already have–plan on adjusting recipe times and sometimes increasing or decreasing the heat. Play around with your cooker and you'll get to know its character.

COOKING BASICS, BY FOOD GROUP

Is your appetite up for some seriously delicious slow cooking? The following guidelines will help smooth the transition from stove top to crockery pot cooking.

Meats and Poultry
- Buy roasts in sizes and shapes that fit your cooker. Otherwise, you'll have to hunt up a meat cleaver and cut them to fit.
- Use lean cuts of meat and poultry for low-fat meals. Before cooking, trim away all visible fat and remove poultry skin.
- Brown ground beef, lamb, chicken, and turkey in a skillet over medium-high heat to give chilies, pasta sauces, and other dishes rich flavor and appealing dark color. To brown the low-fat way, use a nonstick skillet and mist it with a nonstick spray. After the meat is browned, transfer it to the slow cooker, using a slotted spoon so excess fat remains in the skillet.
- Cook cubed beef, chicken, pork, and turkey on LOW for up to 10 hours, but check them after 7 hours. They may be done. For added flavor, brown the cubes before putting them in the slow cooker.

• Add visual appeal and rich braised flavor by browning roasts before cooking them in the slow cooker.

Vegetables

• Place dense root vegetables, such as carrots, turnips, celery root, potatoes, onions, and rutabagas, on the pot bottom, and keep them submerged in the liquid for uniform cooking. Top vegetables with meat (though it's hard to believe, meat cooks faster than the root crops); pour liquids in last.
• Chop vegetables into consistent sizes for even cooking. Bite-size is always good, and ½" × 2" sticks are attractive for Asian-style dishes.
• Stir in frozen peas, cut green beans, and mixed vegetables during the last 15 to 30 minutes of cooking if quantities are small (about ½ cup).
• Add tender vegetables (such as peas and snow peas); strongly flavored vegetables (such as broccoli, brussels sprouts, and cauliflower); and greens (such as kale, spinach, and escarole) during the last 15 to 60 minutes of cooking. Adding large quantities of last-minute goodies will temporarily lower the temperature of the cooking food. Timing depends on how much you're putting in.
• Brown onions and other vegetables to add caramelized color and flavor to dishes. Use the same low-fat techniques described for browning meats and poultry.

Pasta, Rice, and Other Grains

• Use long-grain rices. In slow cooking, they give the fluffiest results.
• Stir in raw rice and barley during the last 1 to 1½ hours of cooking. All-day cooking would result in gummy, almost gelatinous and gloppy grains. Use an extra ¼ cup water for every ¼ cup of raw grain. *Alternate solution:* Cook grains by conventional stove-top and microwave methods; then stir them in during the last 15 minutes. Brown and wild rice buffs take note: The cooking time for brown rice is approximately twice that of white rice. Wild rice takes even longer than brown.
•Add pasta to soups during the last 5 to 10 minutes of cooking. For other dishes, cook pasta on the stove top, then drain it, and top or toss it with the slow cooker ingredients right before serving. Whichever way it's cooked, pasta is best when done al dente.

Dried Beans

•Cooking time varies with bean types and the ingredients cooked with them. Baby limas, great northern beans, and small white beans take less cooking than garbanzos (chick-peas) and kidney beans. Dried beans will roughly double their volume when cooked.

- Boil garbanzo and red kidney beans with three times their volume of water in a large pot on the stove top for 10 minutes. Drain the beans in a colander and discard the water. Add the beans to other ingredients in the slow cooker.
- Soften beans completely before combining them with sweeteners (including brown sugar, honey, maple syrup, and molasses) or acid foods (such as vinegar or tomatoes), which actually harden legumes during cooking. Here's an easy way to do it: Boil beans for 10 minutes, then reduce the heat, cover the pot, and allow the beans to simmer until they're tender, about 1½ hours. Discard the water. Add to ingredients in the slow cooker.

Cheese, Milk, and Other Dairy Products
- Stir cheese, sour cream, yogurt, and cream into main dishes, soups, and stews right before serving. Then cook just long enough to melt the cheese and heat all the ingredients. If cooked for hours, dairy foods tend to separate and look curdled.
- Opt for processed cheeses, which can tolerate heat fairly well, if you must cook cheese for a long period.
- Add milk just before serving, except in dessert recipes created to cook in two to three hours. Milk curdles with lengthy cooking.
- Try canned evaporated skim milk for the longest curdle-free cooking. In many dishes, it makes an excellent low-fat alternative to cream.

Fish
- Stir in shellfish—minced clams, shrimp, scallops—during the last 15 to 60 minutes of cooking, depending on quantity. Shellfish toughens if cooked for long periods.
- Mix in bite-size chunks of sturdy fish such as salmon and shark during the last 30 to 60 minutes of cooking. Cook until done. (To check for doneness, test the fish with a fork. Fully cooked fish should flake easily.)
- Don't use delicate fish such as flounder. It won't hold up during lengthy cooking.

SECRETS TO SUCCESS
Okay, now you've had the basic course in slow cooking. What follows are eight other helpful hints for sure-fire crockery pot success.

- Adjust seasonings at the end of cooking. Some spices, such as black pepper, intensify with lengthy cooking. Others, such as basil and garlic, become diluted and less pungent. Rule of thumb, er...spice: Include whole spices at the beginning of cooking; stir in ground spices and tender herbs at the end. Before serving, taste your creation, and spice it up as desired.
- Garnish dishes for visual pizzazz. Colors fade with lengthy cooking, and a simple garnish can really brighten things up. Here's a handful of off-the-shelf suggestions:

Chopped, seeded tomatoes
Crumbled bacon
Dollop of sour cream, yogurt, or cottage cheese
Fresh grinding of black or white pepper
Grated cheese
Ground nutmeg or ground paprika
Slivered, sliced, or ground nuts
Sprigs or snippings of parsley, cilantro, rosemary, thyme or
  other herbs
Toasted croutons
Wedges or slices of lemon, lime, or orange.

- Use small quantities of liquids when cooking soups. Before serving, thin the soup to an appropriate consistency with water, broth, tomato juice, or milk. Cover and heat on HIGH until hot, 15 to 60 minutes.
- Jump-start cooking by setting the cooker on HIGH for the first hour.
- Resist peeking. Every time you lift the lid, cooking time is extended, because slow cookers aren't designed to crank up the heat when some escapes. These are slow, steady gizmos, from the start of cooking to the finish. Remove the lid only during the last half of cooking and do so only to stir food or check doneness.
- Prepare ingredients ahead, if you want, to make best use of your available time. But be certain to follow the food-safety suggestions in "Safety at Slow Speeds."
- Fill cookers half to three-quarters full, advise manufacturers. Refer to the instructions accompanying your cooker for more information.
- Increase cooking times as necessary if you live at a high altitude.

SAFETY AT SLOW SPEEDS

Food-safety experts assure us that cooking at low temperatures, 200°F (93.3°C) for LOW and 300°F (149°C) for HIGH, is completely safe if you follow these simple, common-sense guidelines:

1. Keep all perishable ingredients in the refrigerator until you're ready to start cooking.
2. Package raw meats and vegetables separately if you're preparing them ahead. You can place either meat or vegetables in the cooker bowl, cover, and refrigerate it, but don't mix the two until you're ready to cook.
3. Never partially cook meat or poultry and finish cooking it later. If you'll be sautéing or browning foods, do so right before adding them to the cooker and turning it on.
4. Check the doneness of roasts with a quick-read thermometer. In a matter of seconds, this handy little gadget will give you a read-out on the meat's internal temperature. The thermometers are available in most cook shops and many large supermarkets.
5. Avoid using large quantities of completely frozen foods in your slow cooker. It's fine to add up to a cup of frozen peas to a potful of hot soup, but starting a recipe with a pound of frozen beef cubes or a frozen turkey breast is a no-no. A slow cooker isn't designed to defrost foods; using it for that purpose can result in gastrointestinal woes. Avoid the risk: Always thaw foods in the refrigerator or microwave; then slow cook them.
6. Refrigerate leftovers quickly—certainly within two hours. If food has been on the table longer than that, don't take a chance. Throw it out. Bacteria thrive at room temperatures.
7. Never reheat foods in a slow cooker. For safety's sake, previously cooked foods should come to a boil quickly. Reheat on the stove top or in a microwave.

KITCHEN WISDOM

Some of the following tips may seem obvious, and others may appear in the manufacturer's instruction booklet, but all bear repeating:

- Avoid sudden temperature changes. Really cold food or water can crack a hot ceramic bowl.
- Always use your slow cooker with the lid on. It's the only way slow cooking works!
- Don't immerse the heating elements in water.

• Turn off or unplug your slow cooker when you are done using it. (Some models have no on/off switch.)

THICKENING SAUCES AND GRAVIES

Is your sauce or gravy thin and watery? That's common with many dishes, including slow-cooked ones. It's up to the cook to make them thick, rich, and smooth. Fortunately, thickening is easy once you know the techniques and the proper proportions of starchy thickener to liquid. For slow-cooked foods, any of the common thickeners work just fine. Choose arrowroot, cornstarch, flour, or tapioca. Here are the specifics on what to do.

Arrowroot and Cornstarch: At the end of cooking, turn the cooker to HIGH. For every 2 cups of liquid in the slow cooker, dissolve 2 tablespoons of arrowroot or cornstarch in 2 tablespoons of *cold water* in a measuring cup. Stir the arrowroot or cornstarch mixture into the food in the slow cooker. Cook for about 5 minutes until the gravy is thick. Don't overstir or overheat. Arrowroot breaks down with too much stirring; cornstarch does with too much heat.

Flour: At the end of cooking, turn the cooker to HIGH. For every 2 cups of liquid in the slow cooker, dissolve 4 tablespoons of instant or regular flour in 4 tablespoons of cold water in a measuring cup. Stir the flour mixture into the food in the slow cooker. Cook about 5 minutes until thick.

Tapioca: At the start of cooking, stir tapioca into the ingredients in the slow cooker. Use *3 to 4* tablespoons of tapioca for every 2 cups of liquid.

Other Thickeners: Potato flakes as well as mashed potatoes, pureed rice, and pureed beans make excellent thickeners. To thicken with them, follow the directions given with individual recipes.

CONVERTING FAMILY FAVORITES

Do you have some favorite soups, stews, and main dishes that you'd like to adapt to slow cooking? Converting recipes is remarkably easy, almost failure-proof, if you follow the slow-cooker guidelines presented here. Read "Cooking Basics" and "Secrets to Success" earlier in this chapter. Apply the techniques discussed there, and make the following adjustments as well.

Liquid: When converting a recipe for slow cooking, reduce the amount of liquid by at least half that required in the conventional recipe. Why? Very little liquid escapes during slow cooking. In fact, condensation forms on the lid, drips back onto the food, and keeps everything nicely moist. A single cup of water, juice, or broth is usually plenty. For soups, use just enough broth or water to cover the ingredients.

Time: When going from stove-top speedy to slow-cooker steady cooking, allow plenty of simmering time. You'll need to experiment with each recipe, but this is the general conversion: Quadruple the conventional cooking time to get the slow-cooker time on LOW. Double the conventional cooking time to get the slow-cooker time on HIGH.

HEALTHFUL COOKING

Whether you're talking slow or conventional cooking, the best ways to decrease fat and sodium are to trim visible fat from meats; remove skin from poultry; add no salt; and cook with as little oil, butter, or margarine as possible.

For high-flavor, low-fat meals, use fatty foods, such as bacon, cheeses, sausage, and nuts in moderate portions. Just a little flavor from these foods can go a long way, as the recipes in this book demonstrate.

And to jazz up foods without salt, use liberal amounts of herbs and spices. Be sure to check the many fresh herbs and chilies available in today's supermarkets, and look for smoke flavorings in the spice section. Another neat trick: Use a couple teaspoons of wine vinegar to give many dishes a flavor boost without the actual sodium.

It's also important to select healthful, tasty alternatives to fatty, salty foods. Read nutritional labels on prepared foods; fats and sodium vary from brand to brand. Check the table on p. 14, which lists some easy-to-find substitutes.

Flavor note: Salt hasn't been added to the recipes. If you prefer saltier flavors, feel free to add salt to taste. Just be aware that ¼ teaspoon of salt packs 533 milligrams (mg) of sodium. Consult the nutritional analysis for each recipe before modifying the amount of salt.

ABOUT THE NUTRITIONAL ANALYSES

In this book, every recipe has a nutritional analysis, which gives today's inquisitive, diet-smart cook information about calories, fat, saturated fat, cholesterol, sodium, and dietary fiber. For most recipes, the analysis reflects a single serving. On an occasional sauce, it's for a specific amount, say ½ cup.

If a food is listed with a substitute ingredient, the analysis was figured using the first choice. For example, if a recipe lists ½ cup frozen peas or corn, the analysis was calculated on the peas. The analysis does not include optional ingredients, garnishes, or variations of ingredients. Analyses were calculated using Nutritionist IV (version 4) for Windows (First DataBank Divison, The Hearst Corporation, 1995).

LOW-FAT AND LOW-SODIUM CHOICES

Choose This	To Replace That
Ground turkey breast meat	Ground beef or hamburger meat
Ground turkey breast meat	Ground turkey
Boneless, skinless chicken breasts	Chicken legs
Fat-free sour cream	Sour cream
Nonfat or low-fat yogurt	Sour cream, cream
Skim milk, evaporated skim milk, and 1% milk	Whole milk, cream
Reduced-fat Cheddar, Swiss, Monterey Jack cheeses	Cheddar, Swiss, Monterey Jack cheeses
Fat-free or light cream cheese	Regular cream cheese
Beans (rinse and drain canned ones to remove as much sodium as possible)	Unrinsed, canned beans
Low-sodium tomato products	Regular tomato products
Fat-free, reduced-sodium broth (chicken and beef)	Regular chicken and beef broth
Low-sodium soy sauce	Regular soy sauce
Garlic powder	Garlic salt
Onion powder, dried minced onions	Onion salt
White wine vinegar, herbs, spices	Table salt

About the Ingredients
Many supermarkets stock seasonings like Thai spice, lemon grass, and 5-spice powder. Can't find them? If you live in a metropolitan area, try looking for them in Hispanic or Asian groceries. Live in a rural area? Consider phoning mail-order merchants listed in the back sections of many popular cooking and lifestyle magazines.

Slow-Simmered Soups

Busy, weary, hungry? Relax with a bowl of hot soup that's ready to eat just when you need a pick-me-up the most. Choose from Fresh Manhattan Clam Chowder, Hearty Kielbasa Soup, Ham and Black Bean Soup with Chilies, Turkey-Noodle Soup, and a potful of favorite others.

Cream of Portobello Mushroom–Barley Soup

This light soup is deliciously flavored with fresh, meaty mushrooms. Serve as a luncheon main course or a dinner first course.

3½- to 4-quart cooker   **Makes 4 servings**

6 ounces portobello mushrooms, chopped into ½-inch cubes

1 medium onion, minced

1 teaspoon tub-style margarine

2 cans (14 ounces each) fat-free beef broth

¼ cup dry sherry

¼ cup barley

¼ teaspoon dried sage

⅛ teaspoon garlic powder

⅛ teaspoon white pepper

1 can (12 ounces) evaporated skim milk

Fresh snipped parsley, for garnish

Sauté the mushrooms and onions in the margarine in a nonstick skillet over medium-high heat, 4 to 5 minutes. Transfer the vegetables to an electric slow cooker. Stir in the broth, sherry, barley, sage, garlic, and pepper. Cover and cook on LOW until the barley is tender, 6 to 8 hours (on HIGH, 4 to 6 hours).

Stir in the milk, and cook until hot, 15 to 30 minutes. Divide the soup among 4 bowls, and garnish each serving with the parsley.

Per serving: About 164 calories, 1.2 g fat (6% of calories), 0.3 g saturated fat, 3.1 mg cholesterol, 252 mg sodium, 2.8 g dietary fiber.

Cook's note: Eight ounces of white button mushrooms, which are less meaty in texture and flavor, can replace the portobellos.

Cream of Scallop Soup

A soup so rich and flavorful you'd think it was laden with butter and cream—but it's not. For a complete meal, pair the soup with a crisp salad.

3½- to 4-quart cooker   **Makes 8 servings**

1 pound potatoes, peeled and cut into ½-inch cubes

¼ cup vegetable broth

2½ cups water

1 tablespoon white wine vinegar

1 medium onion, chopped

1 carrot, finely shredded

¼ teaspoon dried thyme leaves

¼ teaspoon garlic powder

1 egg yolk, lightly beaten

1 cup skim milk

½ pound bay scallops or sea scallops

2 cups shredded reduced-fat Cheddar cheese

Freshly ground black pepper, for garnish

Sprigs of parsley, for garnish

Combine the potatoes, broth, water, vinegar, onions, carrots, thyme, and garlic in an electric slow cooker. Cover and cook on HIGH until the vegetables are tender, 4 to 6 hours (on LOW, 7 to 9 hours). Using a hand-held blender, puree the vegetables.

Add the scallops and cook, covered, for 10 minutes. Stir in the milk and egg yolk. Cook until the soup is hot throughout and the scallops are done, 30 to 60 minutes.

Mix in the cheese and cook until it's melted, about 5 minutes. Divide the soup among 8 bowls, and garnish each serving with the pepper and parsley.

Per serving: About 185 calories, 6 g fat (30% of calories), 3.3 g saturated fat, 59 mg cholesterol, 229 mg sodium, 1.4 g dietary fiber.

Cook's note: If you use sea scallops, halve small ones and quarter large ones.

Cream of Tomato Soup

Move over canned soup . . . this freshly made one rates tasters' choice. Its preparation is almost as simple as the store-bought version—honest.

3½- to 4-quart cooker   **Makes 4 servings**

1 can (28 ounces) plum tomatoes, cut up

1 can (14 ounces) fat-free beef broth

1 medium onion, finely chopped

1 teaspoon butter

1 teaspoon Louisiana hot sauce

½ teaspoon dried thyme leaves

1 teaspoon sugar

½ cup rice

2 teaspoons red wine vinegar

¼ teaspoon black pepper

½ cup half-and-half (or light cream)

Combine the tomatoes, broth, onions, butter, hot sauce, thyme, sugar, rice, vinegar, and pepper in an electric slow cooker. Cover and cook on HIGH for 3½ to 5 hours. Using a hand-held blender, puree the soup. Stir in the half-and-half.

Per serving: About 202 calories, 5.1 g fat (23% of calories), 2.9 g saturated fat, 14 mg cholesterol, 384 mg sodium, 2.5 g dietary fiber.

Cook's note: Fresh out of half-and-half? Substitute canned evaporated skim milk; the taste and texture will be just fine.

Creamy Parsnip-Carrot Soup

A wonderful warmer-upper that gets its mellow, sweet-nutty flavor from parsnips—once as popular as today's ubiquitous potato.

3½- to 4 quart cooker   **Makes 4 servings**

   2 tablespoons rice
   1 pound carrots, peeled and cut into 1-inch cubes
   1 pound parsnips, peeled and cut into 1-inch cubes
   2 cups vegetable broth
   1 cup water
   1 cup evaporated skim milk
   ¼ teaspoon black pepper
   2 tablespoons ground walnuts

Combine the rice, carrots, parsnips, vegetable broth, and water in an electric slow cooker. Cover and cook on LOW until the vegetables are tender, about 5 hours (on HIGH about 3 hours).

Using a hand-held blender, puree the vegetables. Stir in the milk and pepper. Heat the soup until hot, 5 to 10 minutes. Divide the soup among 4 bowls, and sprinkle each serving with 1½ teaspoons of walnuts.

Per serving: About 256 calories, 2.9 g fat (10% of calories), 0.3 g saturated fat, 2.3 mg cholesterol, 168 mg sodium, 8.8 g dietary fiber.

Cook's note: Like their cousins the carrots, the sweetest parsnips are slender and about 8 inches long.

Curried Crookneck Squash Soup
with Ginger

Ginger and curry transform mild crookneck squash into a special taste-bud pleaser. The soup's visually appealing and a terrific source of vitamin A, as well.

3½- to 4-quart cooker   **Makes 8 servings**

1 medium crookneck squash (2½ pounds), peeled and cut into 1-inch cubes

1 medium onion, chopped

1 carrot, coarsely shredded

3 cups fat-free chicken broth

2 teaspoons gingerroot, finely chopped

1 teaspoon curry powder

½ cup half-and-half

Paprika, for garnish

Combine the squash, onions, carrots, and broth in an electric slow cooker. Stir in the gingerroot and curry powder. Cover and cook on LOW until the squash is tender, 7 to 9 hours (on **HIGH**, 4 to 6 hours).

Using a hand-held blender, puree the vegetables. Stir in the half-and-half. Divide the soup among 8 bowls. Swirl in the paprika.

Per serving: About 93 calories, 2.1 g fat (19% of calories), 1.2 g saturated fat, 5.6 mg cholesterol, 141 mg sodium, 0.6 g dietary fiber.

Cook's notes: Popular butternut or acorn squash can replace the crookneck. Don't own a hand-held blender? Mash the vegetables. Or let the soup cool slightly and puree it in batches in a food processor.

Fresh Manhattan Clam Chowder

Never shucked a clam? No problem. Succulent minced clams are readily available in the fish section of most large supermarkets.

5- to 6-quart cooker   **Makes 8 servings**

3 slices bacon

2 celery stalks, finely chopped

3 medium onions, finely chopped

4 small potatoes, diced

2 carrots, diced

½ teaspoon dried thyme leaves

¼ teaspoon black pepper

⅛ teaspoon Louisiana hot sauce, or to taste

1 pint minced clams or 2 cans (6½ ounces each)

1 can (28 ounces) stewed tomatoes, cut up

½ cup snipped fresh parsley

Cook the bacon in a skillet over medium-high heat until it's crisp, about 5 minutes. Drain the bacon on paper towels. Crumble the bacon into an electric slow cooker. Discard the drippings, leaving about 1 teaspoon in the skillet. Sauté the celery and onions in the bacon drippings in the same skillet until golden, 3 to 4 minutes. Transfer the onion mixture to the slow cooker. Stir in the potatoes, carrots, thyme, pepper, and hot sauce.

Drain the liquid from the clams into a pint measuring cup. Add enough water to it to make 2 cups of liquid. Add the clam liquid–water mixture (not the clams) to the slow cooker. Stir in the tomatoes. Cover and cook on LOW for 6 to 8 hours or on HIGH for 4 to 6 hours. During the last hour of cooking, stir in the minced clams. Cover and cook for 1 hour. Stir in the parsley and cook for 15 minutes.

Per serving: About 145 calories, 2.2 g fat (13% of calories), 0.5 g saturated fat, 21 mg cholesterol, 253 mg sodium, 3.3 g dietary fiber.

Cook's notes: Fresh minced clams shouldn't smell fishy. If they do, return them to the store for a truly fresh batch. This chowder will keep for up to 3 days in the refrigerator.

Ham and Black Bean Soup with Chilies

Shredded carrots add a splash of color to this peppery soup.

3½- to 4-quart cooker   **Makes 6 servings**

Nonstick spray

½ pound lean ham, finely chopped

2 cans (14 ounces each) fat-free beef broth

1 can (15 ounces) black beans, rinsed and drained

2 medium onions, chopped

2 medium-hot chili peppers (such as jalapeño, serrano, or poblano), finely chopped

1 large sweet green pepper, chopped

2 carrots, coarsely shredded

1 bay leaf

½ teaspoon cumin seeds

Coat a skillet with nonstick spray and warm it over medium-high heat. Brown the ham, about 5 minutes. Transfer it to an electric slow cooker.

Stir in the broth, beans, onions, chilies, sweet peppers, carrots, bay leaf, and cumin. Cover and cook on LOW for 6 to 8 hours or on HIGH for 4 to 6 hours. Discard the bay leaf.

Per serving: About 182 calories, 2.6 g fat (13% of calories), 0.8 g saturated fat, 21 mg cholesterol, 555 mg sodium, 4.2 g dietary fiber.

Cook's note: If you prefer a less nippy soup, use only 1 medium-hot chili or substitute a mild variety, such as Anaheim.

Hearty Kielbasa Soup

Psyched for the spicy flavor of sausage? It's here in a wonderfully zesty dish that's a snap to make. Serve with sourdough or Russian rye bread.

5- to 6-quart cooker   **Makes 8 servings**

¼ pound light kielbasa, cut in half lengthwise and thinly sliced

1 medium onion, chopped

4 cloves garlic, minced

1 sweet green pepper, chopped

1 celery stalk, thinly sliced

2 cans (14 ounces each) fat-free chicken broth

1 can (15 ounces) stewed tomatoes

1 cup canned pinto beans, rinsed and drained

1 medium carrot, coarsely shredded

1 small zucchini, thinly sliced

¼ cup snipped fresh parsley or 1 tablespoon dried

¼ teaspoon crushed red pepper flakes

¼ teaspoon freshly ground black pepper

Brown the kielbasa in a nonstick skillet over medium-high heat, about 5 minutes. Add the onions, garlic, green pepper, and celery. Sauté until the onions are lightly browned, 1 to 3 minutes.

Transfer the kielbasa mixture to an electric slow cooker. Add the broth, tomatoes, beans, carrots, zucchini, parsley, red and black peppers. Cover and cook on LOW for 7 to 9 hours or on HIGH for 4 to 6 hours.

Per serving: About 185 calories, 3.1 g fat (14% of calories), 0.1 g saturated fat, 0 mg cholesterol, 493 mg sodium, 6.1 g dietary fiber.

Cook's note: This soup is still delicious after a day or two in the refrigerator. Heat on the stove top or in the microwave until hot and bubbly.

Old-World Minestrone with Shell Pasta

Get ready for some hearty and healthful eating; the servings of this classic Italian soup are very generous!

5- to 6-quart cooker   **Makes 4 servings**

1 carrot, shredded

1 celery stalk, sliced

¼ cup frozen peas

1 medium potato, cut into ½-inch cubes

⅔ cup sliced scallions

2 cans (14 ounces each) fat-free chicken or vegetable broth

1 teaspoon Italian herb seasoning or marjoram

1 can (28 ounces) Italian plum tomatoes, cut up

Pinch of cayenne pepper

1 tablespoon red wine vinegar

1 cup chopped escarole

½ cup shell pasta

½ cup snipped fresh parsley

Parmesan cheese (optional)

Combine the carrots, celery, peas, potatoes, scallions, broth, seasoning, tomatoes, pepper, and vinegar in an electric slow cooker. Cover and cook on LOW for 6 to 8 hours or on HIGH for 4 to 5 hours.

During the last 20 minutes of cooking, stir in the escarole and pasta. Divide the soup among 4 bowls, and top each serving with the parsley and cheese, if you wish.

Per serving: About 148 calories, 0.9 g fat (5% of calories), 0.1 g saturated fat, 0 mg cholesterol, 640 mg sodium, 3.9 g dietary fiber.

Cook's note: This vegetable-packed soup is best when freshly made.

Onion-Leek Soup

For a healthful indulgence in French onion soup, be sure to try this slow-simmered version with a Swiss twist.

3½- to 4-quart cooker   **Makes 4 servings**

   2 leeks, white part only, thinly sliced

   3 medium onions, thinly sliced and separated into rings

   1 teaspoon olive oil

   4 cloves garlic, pressed

   1 cup vegetable broth

   3 cups water

   1½ tablespoons white wine vinegar

   2 bay leaves

   4 fresh sage leaves

   ⅛ teaspoon white pepper

   ¼ cup shredded reduced-fat Swiss cheese

   2 cups **garlic croutons**

Sauté the leeks and onions in the oil in a nonstick skillet over medium-high heat until lightly browned. Transfer the vegetables to an electric slow cooker. Stir in the garlic, broth, water, vinegar, bay leaves, sage, and white pepper. Cover and cook on LOW for 6 to 8 hours or on HIGH for 4 to 6 hours. Discard the bay leaves. Divide the soup among 4 bowls, and top each serving with a quarter of the cheese and croutons.

Per serving: About 198 calories, 3.9 g fat (17% of calories), 1.2 g saturated fat, 4.5 mg cholesterol, 199 mg sodium, 3.1 g dietary fiber.

Cook's note: To make 2 cups **garlic croutons,** cut approximately 4 slices of firm bread into ¾-inch cubes. Place the cubes on a baking sheet or a perforated pizza pan. Mist the cubes with nonstick spray, and sprinkle them with garlic powder. Broil them until they're golden, about 5 minutes. Shake or stir the cubes to expose the uncooked sides; broil them until golden, about 3 minutes.

Pimiento-Mushroom Soup

Mushroom aficionados take note: This attractive, light soup goes together almost as fast as you can say pimiento-mushroom.

3½- to 4-quart cooker   **Makes 4 servings**

2 cans (14 ounces each) reduced-fat chicken or vegetable broth

1 tablespoon white wine vinegar

1 bay leaf

8 ounces mushrooms, sliced

2 celery stalks, sliced

2 carrots, sliced

1 jar (4 ounces) pimientos, drained

1 medium onion, chopped

Sprigs of cilantro, for garnish

Combine the broth, vinegar, bay leaf, mushrooms, celery, carrots, pimientos, and onions in an electric slow cooker. Cover and cook on LOW for 6 to 8 hours or on HIGH for 4 to 6 hours. Discard the bay leaf. Divide the soup among 4 bowls, and garnish each serving with the cilantro.

Per serving: About 159 calories, 1.3 g fat (6% of calories), 0.1 g saturated fat, 0 mg cholesterol, 378 mg sodium, 6 g dietary fiber.

Cook's note: This soup keeps nicely in the refrigerator for a day or two.

Potato Cheddar-Cheese Soup

A thick, cheddary soup to die for! Accompany it with vegetable crudités *(carrots, celery, cauliflower, sweet red pepper and broccoli) and serve chocolate chip muffins for dessert.*

3½- to 4-quart cooker   **Makes 4 servings**

6 large or 10 medium potatoes, peeled and cut into 1-inch cubes

½ cup low-sodium vegetable broth

1 cup water

1 large onion, finely chopped

½ teaspoon garlic powder

⅛ teaspoon white pepper

2 cups skim milk

1 cup shredded sharp or extra-sharp Cheddar cheese

Paprika, for garnish

Place the potatoes, broth, water, onions, and garlic powder in an electric slow cooker. Cover and cook on LOW until the potatoes are tender, 7 to 9 hours (on HIGH, 4 to 6 hours).

Using a potato masher or a hand-held blender, mash the potatoes, stirring in the pepper and the milk a little at a time. Mix in the cheese and cook until the cheese has melted, about 5 minutes. Add more milk if needed. Divide the soup among 4 bowls; garnish each serving with paprika.

Per serving: About 350 calories, 10 g fat (25% of calories), 6.2 g saturated fat, 32 mg cholesterol, 265 mg sodium, 4 g dietary fiber.

Cook's note: Nonfat Cheddar cheese will work in this recipe, but it won't have the flavor impact.

Potato and Leek Soup with Ham

A little ham adds lots of texture and flavor to this comforting soup. For some crunch, serve with melba toast.

3½- to 4-quart cooker   **Makes 8 servings**

Nonstick spray

6 ounces ham, cut into ¼-inch cubes

2 large leeks, white parts only, thinly sliced

4 large potatoes, peeled and finely shredded

2 cans (14 ounces each) fat-free chicken broth

⅛ teaspoon black pepper

1 cup skim milk

8 ounces nonfat ricotta cheese

Snipped fresh parsley

Coat a skillet with nonstick spray and warm it over medium-high heat. Add the ham, and cook it until lightly browned, about 5 minutes. Add the leeks, and cook until they're translucent, 3 to 4 minutes. Transfer the ham and leeks to an electric slow cooker.

Stir in the potatoes, broth, and pepper. Cover and cook on LOW until the potatoes are tender, 6 to 8 hours (on HIGH, 4 to 6 hours). Stir well to break up the potatoes.

Stir in the milk and cheese, and cook until the soup is hot, 5 to 15 minutes. Divide the soup among 8 bowls, and garnish each serving with the parsley.

Per serving: About 151 calories, 1.5 g (9% of calories), 0.5 g saturated fat, 12 mg cholesterol, 476 mg sodium, 1.7 g dietary fiber.

Cook's notes: Shredding the potatoes before cooking eliminates the need for mashing them afterward. Though best when served fresh, this soup will keep for a day in the refrigerator.

Rutabaga Soup with Nutmeg

The Swedish turnip or rutabaga, once known as the swede, plus some potatoes equal an outstanding creamy soup.

3½- to 4-quart cooker   **Makes 8 servings**

2 medium onions, chopped

1 stalk celery, chopped

3 cups of 1-inch cubes of peeled potatoes

2 cups of 1-inch cubes of peeled rutabagas

2 cans (14 ounces each) fat-free chicken broth

2 cloves garlic, minced

⅛ teaspoon white pepper

⅓ cup skim milk

1 teaspoon ground nutmeg

Snipped fresh flat parsley, for garnish

Combine the onions, celery, potatoes, rutabagas, broth, garlic, and pepper in an electric slow cooker. Cover and cook on HIGH until the vegetables are tender, 4 to 6 hours. Using a hand-held blender, puree the vegetables. Stir in the milk.

Divide the soup among 8 bowls. Sprinkle each serving with ⅛ teaspoon nutmeg, and garnish with the parsley.

Per serving: About 108 calories, 0.2 g fat (2% of calories), 0.1 g saturated fat, 0.2 mg cholesterol, 188 mg sodium, 2.8 g dietary fiber.

Cook's note: If rutabagas aren't readily available, substitute white turnips.

Salmon, Corn, and Red Pepper Chowder

Celebrate fresh salmon season with this spicy chowder, which is a meal in itself. And by the way, the vitamin C's high, thanks to potatoes and sweet red peppers.

5- to 6-quart cooker   **Makes 6 servings**

3 cups corn

3 medium sweet red peppers, coarsely chopped

2 medium red potatoes, cut into ¾-inch cubes

1 medium onion, chopped

1 can (14 ounces) vegetable broth

1 cup water

2 fresh chili peppers, minced

4 cloves garlic, minced

2 tablespoons white wine vinegar

1 tablespoon chili powder

1 teaspoon cumin seed

1 teaspoon dried oregano

½ pound salmon steak, bones removed and cut into 1½-inch cubes

Combine the corn, sweet peppers, potatoes, onions, vegetable broth, and water in an electric slow cooker. Stir in the chili peppers, garlic, vinegar, chili powder, cumin, and oregano. Carefully stir in the salmon. Cover and cook on LOW until the vegetables are tender and the salmon is cooked through, 6 to 8 hours.

Per serving: About 272 calories, 4.8 g fat (15% of calories), 0.9 g saturated fat, 22 mg cholesterol, 64 mg sodium, 2.4 g dietary fiber.

Cook's note: For a chowder with less chili fire, use only 1 fresh chili pepper and 1½ teaspoons of chili powder.

Shrimp-Rice Soup

A light, delicately seasoned soup that makes a delicious first course—perfect for a luncheon or dinner.

3½- to 4-quart cooker   **Makes 4 servings**

2 cans (14 ounces each) fat-free chicken broth

1 small onion, finely chopped

1 celery stalk, thinly sliced

⅛ teaspoon white pepper

¼ cup brown rice

½ pound medium shrimp, shelled, deveined and cut into thirds

Combine the broth, onion, celery, pepper, and rice in an electric slow cooker. Cover and cook on LOW for 6 to 8 hours or on HIGH for 4 to 6 hours. During the last hour of cooking, stir in the shrimp. Cover and cook until the shrimp are cooked through and tender, about 1 hour.

Per serving: About 129 calories, 1.3 g fat (9% of calories), 0.3 g saturated fat, 86 mg cholesterol, 397 mg sodium, 0.5 g dietary fiber.

Cook's note: To make **Chicken-Rice Soup,** replace the shrimp with cubed chicken breast. Add the chicken along with the broth and other ingredients.

Smoky Pinto Bean and Potato Soup

Here's a serious hunger-stopper that's packed with fiber-rich potatoes, carrots and beans, and intriguing cumin-mesquite flavor, as well.

3½- to 4-quart cooker   **Makes 6 servings**

1 medium onion, chopped

2 medium red potatoes, cut into ½-inch cubes

2 carrots, thinly sliced

1 celery stalk, thinly sliced

1 can (14 ounces) pinto beans, rinsed and drained

2 cans (14 ounces each) fat-free beef broth

2 cloves garlic, chopped

½ teaspoon cumin seed

¼ teaspoon black pepper

1 teaspoon mesquite smoke flavoring

1 tablespoon white wine vinegar

¼ pound chopped smoked sausage (optional)

Combine the onions, potatoes, carrots, celery, beans, sausage, if you wish, and broth in an electric slow cooker. Stir in the garlic, cumin, pepper, smoke flavoring, and vinegar. Cover and cook on HIGH until the vegetables are tender, 3½ to 5 hours.

Per serving: About 137 calories, 1.7 g fat (11% of calories), 0.3 g saturated fat, 0 mg cholesterol, 236 mg sodium, 4.2 g dietary fiber.

Southwest Chicken and Corn Chowder

Lots of cream-style corn combines with chicken and potatoes for a pleasingly chunky chowder. Cumin and jalapeño pepper provide the distinctive southwest flavor. Olé!

3½- to 4-quart cooker   **Makes 8 servings**

1 can (14 ounces) fat-free chicken broth

1 pound boneless, skinless chicken breast, cut into ¾-inch cubes

1 medium sweet red pepper, chopped

1 medium sweet green pepper, chopped

1 medium onion, chopped

2 cloves garlic, minced

2 cans (8 ounces each) low-sodium cream-style corn

2 medium potatoes, cut into ½-inch cubes

1 cup frozen corn

1 teaspoon cumin seeds

1 dried cayenne pepper, minced

2 tablespoons cornstarch

½ cup evaporated skim milk

Combine the broth, chicken, sweet peppers, onions, garlic, cream-style corn, potatoes, frozen corn, cumin, and cayenne in an electric slow cooker. Cover and cook on LOW until the chicken is tender and cooked through, 8 to 10 hours.

In a measuring cup, mix the cornstarch and milk until blended. Pour into the chicken soup and cook until it is slightly thickened.

Per serving: About 221 calories, 2.8 g fat (11% of calories), 0.7 g saturated fat, 49 mg cholesterol, 143 mg sodium, 2 g dietary fiber.

Cook's note: If cumin seeds and a dried cayenne pepper aren't on hand, use ¾ teaspoon ground cumin and 1 teaspoon crushed red pepper flakes instead.

Summer Squash Soup with Lemon Grass

Lemon grass imparts an enticing lemony fragrance to this pleasantly nippy yet delicate Thai-spiced soup.

3½- to 4-quart cooker   **Makes 4 servings**

1 can (14 ounces) Oriental broth or chicken or vegetable broth

2 cups water

2 small zucchini, halved lengthwise and sliced

1 medium yellow squash, halved lengthwise and sliced

1 leek, white part only, sliced

1 medium onion, halved lengthwise and thinly sliced

3 cloves garlic, pressed

1 stalk lemon grass, halved

½ teaspoon Thai seasoning

¼ teaspoon crushed red pepper flakes

6 medium kale leaves, chopped

Combine the broth, water, zucchini, squash, leek, onion, garlic, lemon grass, Thai seasoning, and pepper flakes in an electric slow cooker. Cover and cook on LOW for 5 to 9 hours or on HIGH for 3½ to 5 hours. Discard the lemon grass. Stir in the kale. Cover and cook until the kale is wilted, 5 to 10 minutes.

Per serving: About 73 calories, 0.6 g fat (6% of calories), 0.1 g saturated fat, 0 mg cholesterol, 538 mg sodium, 2.9 g dietary fiber.

Cook's note: Lemon grass is available in Asian specialty markets and many supermarkets. If you can't find any, substitute a 2-inch piece of lemon peel.

Thymely Vegetable Soup with Ziti

Here's a dish with plenty of herbal flavor and just the right amount of zip. Serve with crusty rustic or French bread.

5- to 6-quart cooker   **Makes 4 servings**

2 cups water

1 medium onion, chopped

½ cup dried lentils, rinsed

1 small carrot, thinly sliced

¼ teaspoon celery seed

1½ teaspoons brown sugar

¼ teaspoon dried marjoram

¼ teaspoon dried thyme leaves

⅛ teaspoon freshly ground black pepper

2 cloves garlic, minced

1 can (14 ounces) fat-free chicken or vegetable broth

1 can (15 ounces) crushed tomatoes

½ medium zucchini, cut in half lengthwise and thinly sliced

½ cup frozen corn

2 tablespoons white wine vinegar

½ cup ziti

½ cup grated Parmesan or Romano cheese

Mix the water, onions, lentils, carrots, and celery seed in an electric slow cooker. Stir in the sugar, marjoram, thyme, pepper, garlic, broth, tomatoes, zucchini, corn, and vinegar. Cover and cook on LOW for 6 to 8 hours or on HIGH for 4 to 5 hours. During the last hour of cooking, stir in the ziti. Cover and cook until the ziti are al dente, 10 to 30 minutes. Divide the soup among 4 bowls, and sprinkle each serving with 2 tablespoons of the cheese.

Per serving: About 288 calories, 4.4 g fat (14% of calories), 2.5 g saturated fat, 10 mg cholesterol, 659 mg sodium, 3.5 g dietary fiber.

Cook's note: This soup is best when served freshly made.

Tomato-Basil Soup with Ditalini

A hearty tomato classic that packs plenty of flavor and uses small pasta instead of rice.

3½- to 4-quart cooker   **Makes 4 servings**

1 can (28 ounces) crushed tomatoes

1 clove garlic, minced

1 small onion, finely chopped

1 small carrot, finely shredded

1 celery stalk, thinly sliced

¾ cup vegetable broth

1 teaspoon sugar

1 bay leaf

1 tablespoon dry sherry

⅛ teaspoon black pepper

4 fresh basil leaves, snipped

1 cup ditalini or orzo

1 cup evaporated skim milk

Combine tomatoes, garlic, onions, carrots, celery, broth, sugar, bay leaf, sherry, and pepper in an electric slow cooker. Cover and cook on LOW for 6 to 8 hours or on HIGH for 4 to 6 hours. Discard bay leaf.

Stir in the basil and ditalini. Cover and cook for 10 minutes. Stir in milk. Cover and cook until the ditalini are tender and the soup hot, 5 to 30 minutes.

Per serving: About 250 calories, 0.7 g fat (2% of calories), 0.2 g saturated fat, 2.3 mg cholesterol, 458 mg sodium, 4.3 g dietary fiber.

Cook's note: Ditalini cook quickly; be careful not to overcook.

Tomato-Cheese Tortellini Soup

Stuffed pasta gets a "souper" role in this robust one-dish meal.

3½- to 4-quart cooker   **Makes 8 servings**

1 can (28 ounces) whole plum tomatoes, cut up

2 cans (14 ounces each) vegetable broth or fat-free chicken broth

1 cup sliced scallions

1 cup chopped fresh or frozen green peppers

½ teaspoon dried oregano

1 tablespoon snipped fresh basil or ½ teaspoon dried

1 tablespoon white wine vinegar

2 cups (1 pound) frozen tricolor cheese tortellini

Combine the tomatoes, broth, scallions, peppers, oregano, basil, and vinegar in an electric slow cooker. Cover and cook on LOW for 6 to 8 hours or on HIGH for 4 to 5 hours.

During the last hour of cooking, stir in the tortellini. Cover and cook until the tortellini are tender and hot, about 75 minutes.

Per serving: About 220 calories, 7.7 g fat (31% of calories), 4 g saturated fat, 50 mg cholesterol, 402 mg sodium, 1.8 g dietary fiber.

Cook's notes: Fresh tortellini will also work in this recipe; allow 45 to 60 minutes for them to cook. The soup is best eaten fresh, but will keep for up to 3 days in the refrigerator.

Tomato-Tortilla Soup

Crisp flat-bread tops a peppery-hot, south-of-the-border-style soup. Get ready for a superb, palate-stimulating experience!

3½- to 4-quart cooker   **Makes 6 servings**

4 cups crushed tomatoes

1¼ cups vegetable broth

2 medium onions, finely chopped

3 cloves garlic, minced

2 dried cayenne peppers, minced, or 2 teaspoons crushed red pepper flakes

1 tablespoon dried parsley

6 corn tortillas, cut into ¾-inch strips

Nonstick olive oil spray

1 cup (4 ounces) shredded Monterey Jack cheese

Combine the tomatoes, broth, onions, garlic, peppers, and parsley in an electric slow cooker. Cover and cook on LOW for 7 to 9 hours or on HIGH for 3½ to 5 hours.

Place the tortillas on a baking sheet, and mist them with the olive oil spray. Broil them until they're crisp and golden, about 5 minutes.

Divide the soup among 6 bowls, and top each serving with tortilla strips and cheese.

Per serving: About 210 calories, 6.6 g fat (28% of calories), 3.7 g saturated fat, 17 mg cholesterol, 421 mg sodium, 3.7 g dietary fiber.

Cook's note: Toasted flour tortillas or crisp, broken taco shells can replace the corn tortillas.

Turkey-Noodle Soup

Try this soul-warming soup that hits the spot on a cold winter's day. Serve with warm buttermilk biscuits and tossed vegetable salad.

3½- to 4-quart cooker   **Makes 4 servings**

2 cans (14 ounces each) fat-free chicken broth

1 celery stalk, thinly sliced

1 carrot, thinly sliced

1 medium onion, finely chopped

½ pound turkey breast, cut into ¾-inch cubes

⅛ teaspoon white pepper

½ teaspoon dried thyme leaves

1 tablespoon white wine vinegar

1 cup medium noodles

½ cup peas

Combine the broth, celery, carrots, onions, turkey, pepper, thyme, and vinegar in an electric slow cooker. Cover and cook on LOW until the turkey is tender, 7 to 9 hours (on HIGH, 4 to 6 hours).

Stir in the noodles and peas. Cover and cook until the peas and noodles are done, 5 to 10 minutes.

Per serving: About 175 calories, 1 g fat (5% of calories), 0.3 g saturated fat, 56 mg cholesterol, 353 mg sodium, 1.8 g dietary fiber.

Cook's note: Chicken breast with thin noodles makes a tasty variation on this dish.

White Bean Soup du Jour

Tomatoes, parsley, and croutons create a medley of colors and textures atop this smooth, sophisticated cream-and-bean soup.

3½- to 4-quart cooker   **Makes 4 servings**

1 can (16 ounces) great northern beans, rinsed and drained

1 medium onion, quartered

2 cloves garlic, pressed

1 carrot, shredded

1 stalk celery, finely chopped

1 teaspoon dried thyme leaves

1 can (14 ounces) fat-free chicken broth

½ cup half-and-half

2 plum tomatoes, seeded and chopped

Snipped fresh parsley, for garnish

Garlic Croutons for garnish (see page 25)

Combine the beans, onions, garlic, carrots, celery, thyme, and broth in an electric slow cooker. Cover and cook on LOW for 6 to 8 hours or on HIGH for 3½ to 5 hours.

Using a hand-held blender or a food processor, puree the bean soup. Stir in the half-and-half. Divide the soup among 4 bowls; top each serving with the tomatoes. Garnish with the parsley and **Garlic Croutons.**

Per serving: About 240 calories, 4.1 g fat (15% of calories), 2.3 g saturated fat, 11 mg cholesterol, 190 mg sodium, 7.1 g dietary fiber.

Cook's note: To seed the tomatoes, cut them in half, and gently squeeze out the seeds and pulp.

Hearty Stews

If you've never made a stew, this is a good place to start. These one-dish meals are forgiving (they adapt readily to a pinch more or less of spice, a potato more or less) and go together in mere minutes. Savor mouth-watering Beef Bourguignon, Hungarian-Style Goulash, Rustic Chicken Stew, Superb Shrimp and Sausage Stew, and many more.

Beef Bourguignon

Like the classic French version, this rendition simmers beef in a hearty Burgundy wine, flavored with an aromatic bouquet garni. Serve over split baked potatoes, which soak up the wonderful broth, or dip into it with a side helping of crusty French bread.

5- to 6-quart cooker   **Makes 12 servings**

½ cup flour

3 pounds beef rump roast, cut into 1-inch cubes

2 strips of bacon

1 teaspoon olive oil

6 tablespoons fat-free beef broth

1 package (16 ounces) frozen pearl onions

¾ cup Burgundy wine

Bouquet garni (celery stalk, thyme sprig, bay leaf, parsley sprig, and sage leaves, wrapped in cheesecloth)

Freshly ground black pepper

Place the flour in a clean paper bag, add the beef cubes, and gently shake the bag to coat them with the flour.

Cook the bacon in a nonstick skillet over medium-high heat until crisp, 3 to 5 minutes. Drain the strips on paper towels and crumble them. Using paper towels, wipe the skillet to remove excess fat.

Brown the beef in the same skillet over medium-high heat, adding the olive oil and broth as necessary to aid browning and to prevent sticking. Transfer the beef to an electric slow cooker.

In the same skillet as used before, quickly brown the onions, adding broth as needed to prevent sticking and to help loosen pieces of browned meat and flour. Cook for 1 to 2 minutes. Transfer the onions and pan scrapings to the slow cooker.

Stir in the Burgundy and add the bouquet garni. Sprinkle the beef and onion mixture with the pepper and crumbled bacon. Cover and cook on LOW until the meat and onions are tender, 8 to 10 hours. Discard the bouquet garni.

Per serving: About 218 calories, 6 g fat (25% of calories), 1.9 g saturated fat, 61 mg cholesterol, 135 mg sodium, 0.8 g dietary fiber.

Cook's notes: To make a bouquet garni, tie fresh celery, thyme, bay leaf, parsley, and sage together with kitchen string. Or tie dried celery seed, thyme leaves, bay leaf, parsley flakes, and sage together in a small cheesecloth sack.

This dish freezes well for up to 1 month. To reheat, thaw it in the refrigerator, and cook until it's hot and bubbling throughout.

Bratwurst Simmered in Beer

This is an absolutely delicious "wurst" case cooking event.

5- to 6-quart cooker   **Makes 4 servings**

½ pound bratwurst, sliced ½ inch thick

4 medium potatoes, peeled and sliced ½ inch thick

3 parsnips, peeled and cut into 2-inch cubes

3 medium onions, quartered

1 bottle (12 ounces) Oktoberfest-style beer

Brown the bratwurst in a nonstick skillet over medium-high heat. Transfer it to an electric slow cooker.

In the same skillet, brown the potatoes, parsnips, and onions. Transfer the vegetables to the slow cooker. Pour in the beer. Cover and cook on LOW until the meat is done and the vegetables are tender, 6 to 8 hours.

Per serving: About 261 calories, 10 g fat (34% of calories), 3.6 g saturated fat, 23 mg cholesterol, 225 mg sodium, 4.6 g dietary fiber.

Cook's note: Fully cooked sausage needs less cooking time.

Hungarian-Style Goulash

Known as gulyás *in its native Hungary, this stew releases tantalizing aromas as browned beef simmers in a spicy mixture of mushrooms, onions, tomatoes and paprika. Serve with a simple green salad or steamed peas.*

5- to 6-quart cooker   **Makes 8 servings**

Nonstick spray

2 pounds beef rump roast, trimmed of fat and cut into 1½-inch cubes

6 medium onions, halved lengthwise and thinly sliced

2 cups chopped portobello mushrooms

½ cup water

1 tablespoon paprika

¼ teaspoon black pepper

1 teaspoon browning sauce

2½ cups diced tomatoes or 1 can (14 ounce) crushed tomatoes

16 ounces broad noodles

Caraway seeds, for garnish

Coat a nonstick skillet with nonstick spray, and warm it over medium heat. Add the beef and cook it until well-browned on all sides, 4 to 6 minutes. Transfer the beef to an electric slow cooker.

Add the onions and mushrooms to the same skillet, and sauté them until the onions are translucent, 3 to 5 minutes. Transfer the onion-mushroom mixture to the slow cooker. Pour the water into the skillet and bring it to a boil, scraping the skillet to remove the brown drippings.

Pour the liquid into the slow cooker. Add the paprika, pepper, browning sauce and tomatoes to the slow cooker. Mix well. Cover and cook on LOW until the beef is tender, 8 to 10 hours. When the goulash is done, boil the noodles in water and drain. Serve the goulash over hot noodles and garnish each serving with a sprinkling of caraway.

Per serving: About 364 calories, 10 g fat (25% of calories), 3.2 g. saturated fat, 101 mg cholesterol, 210 mg sodium, 4.1 g dietary fiber.

Cook's notes: Goulash, minus the noodles, can be frozen for up to a month. To reheat, thaw it in the refrigerator, and cook until it's hot and bubbly throughout. Keep leftover noodles for just a day or two in the refrigerator. Refresh them in boiling water.

Ratatouille with Feta Cheese

Mediterranean style: This old-world favorite is full to the brim with eggplant and fresh basil flavors. Few dishes adapt better to unattended slow cooking.

5- to 6-quart cooker   **Makes 4 servings**

1 cup fat-free beef broth

1 cup crushed tomatoes

1 can (16 ounces) stewed tomatoes

2 medium onions, halved and sliced

1 medium zucchini, thinly sliced

3/4 pound eggplant, peeled and cut into 3/4-inch cubes

4 cloves garlic, minced

1 yellow pepper, thinly sliced

1 teaspoon white wine vinegar

2 sprigs of lemon thyme

6 leaves fresh basil, snipped

2 ounces feta cheese, crumbled

Combine the broth, tomatoes, and stewed tomatoes in an electric slow cooker. Stir in the onions, zucchini, eggplant, garlic, pepper, and vinegar. Add the lemon thyme. Cover and cook on LOW for 6 to 8 hours or on HIGH for 4 to 6 hours. Discard the lemon thyme and stir in the basil. Divide the stew among 4 bowls and sprinkle feta cheese over each serving.

Per serving: About 159 calories, 3.8 g fat (20% of calories), 2.2 g saturated fat, 12 mg cholesterol, 528 mg sodium, 3.4 g dietary fiber.

Cook's note: No lemon thyme available? Substitute a sprig of thyme and a strip of lemon peel.

Asian Stir-Fry Stew

When you want the flavor of a stir-fry, but not the last-minute fuss, give this easily prepared stew a try.

3½- to 4-quart cooker   **Makes 4 servings**

1 cup Oriental broth, chicken, or vegetable broth

2 medium carrots, cut into ¾-inch cubes

1 tablespoon minced gingerroot

1 clove garlic, minced

1 can (15 ounces) baby corn, drained

1 cup sliced scallions

1 can (8 ounces) sliced water chestnuts

1 can (14 ounces) bean sprouts

¾ pound bok choy, chopped

½ pound bay scallops

1 teaspoon sesame oil

10 ounces Chinese wheat noodles

Low-sodium soy sauce (optional)

1 tablespoon powdered hot mustard (optional)

Mix the broth, carrots, gingerroot, garlic, corn, scallions, chestnuts, and bean sprouts in an electric slow cooker. Cover and cook on LOW for 5 hours. Add the bok choy. Cover and cook for 15 minutes. Stir in the scallops and sesame oil. Cover and cook until the scallops are done, about 30 minutes. Boil the noodles in water and drain. Serve the stew over the noodles. Sprinkle with the optional soy sauce. Serve with the **hot mustard** for dipping, if you wish.

Per serving: About 467 calories, 6 g fat (10% of calories), 1 g saturated fat, 78 mg cholesterol, 474 mg sodium, 7 g dietary fiber.

Cook's note: To make **hot mustard,** combine 1 tablespoon powdered mustard with enough cold water to make a paste. Let the mixture stand for 10 minutes; then use with caution. This mustard packs the power to scorch your sinuses!

Moroccan Lamb Stew with Couscous

This palate-pleasing North African stew features coriander-seasoned meatballs in a tomato-apricot-currant sauce—an intriguing blend of bold spices and sweet fruit.

5- to 6-quart cooker   **Makes 12 servings**

1 pound lean ground lamb

1/3 cup quick oats

1/3 cup dried parsley

1/3 cup dried minced onion

1/2 teaspoon ground coriander

1/8 teaspoon black pepper

1/8 teaspoon ground cinnamon

1/8 teaspoon ground nutmeg

4 cloves garlic, minced

1/2 teaspoon cumin seed

1 dried cayenne pepper, minced

2 pounds tomatoes, chopped

3/4 cup chopped dried apricots

1/2 cup dried currants

1 cup couscous

Combine the lamb, oats, parsley, onions, coriander, pepper, cinnamon, and nutmeg. Shape into 1- × 2-inch meatballs, and brown in a nonstick skillet over medium-high heat.

Mix the garlic, cumin, cayenne, tomatoes, apricots, and currants in an electric slow cooker. Add the meatballs, cover, and cook on LOW until the lamb is cooked through and the apricots are tender, 7 to 9 hours. In a saucepan, bring 2 cups of water to a boil; stir in the couscous. Cover and remove from heat and allow to stand for 5 minutes. Serve stew over the hot couscous.

Per serving: About 178 calories, 3.3 g fat (16% of calories), 1.1 g saturated fat, 26 mg cholesterol, 33 mg sodium, 5.1 g dietary fiber.

Old-Fashioned Pound Stew

Here's a simple, home-style stew like grandmom used to make. It uses a pound each of carrots, potatoes, onions, tomatoes, and beef.

5- to 6-quart cooker   **Makes 8 servings**

1 pound lean beef cubes

¼ cup unbleached flour

½ teaspoon olive oil

1 pound carrots, cut diagonally into 1-inch-thick pieces

1 pound potatoes, cut into 1-inch cubes

1 pound plum tomatoes, chopped

1 pound frozen pearl onions

⅛ teaspoon black pepper

1¼ cups water

2 cups frozen peas

Basic Wheat Dumplings (see page 96)

3 teaspoons browning sauce

2 tablespoons cornstarch

Dredge the beef in the flour, then brown the pieces on all sides in the oil in a nonstick skillet over medium-high heat, about 5 minutes. Transfer the beef to an electric slow cooker. Add the carrots, potatoes, tomatoes, pearl onions, pepper, and 1 cup of water; mix. Cover and cook on LOW until the vegetables and beef cubes are tender, 8 to 10 hours. Stir in the peas. Cover and and cook for 15 minutes.

Turn the heat to HIGH, and drop in the dumplings. Cover and cook until they're done, about 30 minutes. Transfer the dumplings to a plate and keep them warm.

In a measuring cup, mix the cornstarch, the remaining ¼ cup of water, and browning sauce. Pour it into the stew, mix well, and heat until the liquid is thickened. Serve the stew over the dumplings.

Per serving: About 238 calories, 3.4 g fat (13% of calories), 1 g saturated fat, 30 mg cholesterol, 177 mg sodium, 5.2 g dietary fiber.

Cook's note: If pearl onions aren't available, use yellow onions and cut them into wedges.

Rustic Chicken Stew

This chunky stew is easy to make and features chicken, carrots, corn, and peas—all tastefully seasoned with thyme.

5- to 6-quart cooker   **Makes 8 servings**

2 pounds boneless, skinless chicken breasts, cut into 1-inch cubes

3 medium onions, quartered

2 carrots, cut into 1-inch-thick slices

2 potatoes, cut into 1-inch cubes

2 cans (14 ounces each) fat-free chicken broth

1 teaspoon celery seed

1 teaspoon dried thyme leaves

½ teaspoon black pepper

8 ounces mushrooms, halved

1 cup frozen corn

1 cup frozen peas

Combine the chicken, onions, carrots, potatoes, and broth in an electric slow cooker. Stir in the celery seed, thyme, pepper, mushrooms, and corn. Cover and cook on LOW until the chicken is done and the vegetables are tender, 7 to 9 hours (or on HIGH 4 to 6 hours). Stir in the peas and cook until they're done, 15 to 30 minutes.

Per serving: About 295 calories, 4.6 g fat (14% of calories), 1.2 g saturated fat, 96 mg cholesterol, 249 mg sodium, 3.4 g dietary fiber.

Cook's note: Baby carrots make a quick and easy substitute for the 1-inch-thick carrot slices.

Sausage and Butternut Squash Stew

This deliciously earthy stew is great for chasing the chills on a nippy fall day. Serve with slices of hearty oat bread.

3½- to 4-quart cooker   **Makes 4 servings**

   1½ pound butternut squash, peeled and cut into ¾-inch cubes

   1 medium potato, cut into ½-inch cubes

   2 slender carrots, sliced diagonally ¾-inch thick, or 12 baby carrots

   1 cup frozen cut green beans

   1 can (14 ounces) fat-free beef broth

   1 tablespoon red wine vinegar

   ¼ teaspoon black pepper

   1 teaspoon dried rosemary, crushed

   ¼ pound low-fat turkey sausage or light kielbasa, cut in half lengthwise and thickly sliced

   4 small onions, halved

   ¼ cup cold water

   2 tablespoons cornstarch

   Snipped fresh parsley, for garnish

Combine the squash, potatoes, carrots, beans, broth, vinegar, pepper, and rosemary in an electric slow cooker.

Brown the sausage in a skillet over medium-high heat; add the onions and cook until the onions are lightly browned, about 4 minutes. Transfer the sausage and onions to the slow cooker. Cover and cook on LOW until the vegetables are tender and the flavors have blended, 6 to 8 hours. In a measuring cup, mix the water and cornstarch, and pour the mixture into the stew. Mix well and heat until the liquid has thickened. Garnish with the parsley.

Per serving: About 234 calories, 3 g fat (11% of calories), 0.8 g saturated fat, 18 mg cholesterol, 629 mg sodium, 6.2 g dietary fiber.

Cook's note: Butternut squash is a hard vegetable with a hard rind. For easiest cutting, use a sharp, sturdy French chef's knife and work on a firm work surface.

Shrimp and Mako Shark Gumbo

Gumbo wouldn't be gumbo without okra, the king of vegetables in bayou country. Our easy-cooking gumbo uses mako shark, but you can substitute catfish, if you wish.

5- to 6-quart cooker   **Makes 6 servings**

1 medium onion, finely chopped

2 celery stalks, thinly sliced

1 teaspoon butter

1 can (14 ounces) fat-free chicken broth

1 sweet green pepper, chopped

8 ounces okra, sliced, or 1 package (10 ounces) frozen

2 cloves garlic, minced

1 can (28 ounces) whole tomatoes, cut up

½ teaspoon Louisiana hot sauce, or to taste

2 bay leaves

½ pound medium shrimp, shelled and deveined

½ pound mako shark steak, cut into 1-inch cubes

2¼ cups rice

Sauté the onions and celery in the butter in a nonstick skillet over medium-high heat until translucent. Transfer the vegetables to an electric slow cooker.

Stir in the broth, green peppers, okra, garlic, tomatoes, hot sauce, and bay leaves. Cover and cook on LOW for 7 to 9 hours or on HIGH for 3½ to 5 hours. In the last half-hour, cook the rice separately; keep it warm.

Meanwhile, gently stir the shrimp and mako into the gumbo in the slow cooker. Cover and cook on HIGH until the shrimp and mako are cooked through, 30 to 60 minutes. Serve over the hot cooked rice.

Per serving: About 412 calories, 4.1 g fat (9% of calories), 1.1 g saturated fat, 78 mg cholesterol, 225 mg sodium, 3.7 g dietary fiber.

Spicy Three-Bean Stew

Fabulous flavor and lots of fiber characterize this vegetarian main course. It's a meal in itself.

5- to 6-quart cooker   **Makes 8 servings**

1 can (28 ounces) whole plum tomatoes, cut up

1 can (15 ounces) red kidney beans, rinsed and drained

1 can (15 ounces) black beans, rinsed and drained

1 can (15 ounces) pinto beans, rinsed and drained

1 cup corn

½ cup brown rice

6 cloves garlic, chopped

3 medium onions, quartered and separated

2 medium sweet red peppers, cut into thin strips

1 tablespoon chili powder

1 teaspoon ground cumin

¼ teaspoon ground allspice

¼ teaspoon ground coriander

1 tablespoon red wine vinegar

Combine the tomatoes, beans, corn, rice, garlic, onions, red peppers, chili powder, cumin, allspice, coriander, and vinegar in an electric slow cooker. Cover and cook on LOW for 7 to 9 hours or on HIGH for 4 to 6 hours.

Per serving: About 307 calories, 1.7 g fat (4% of calories), 0.3 g saturated fat, 0 mg cholesterol, 214 mg sodium, 12.1 g dietary fiber.

Cook's note: This hearty stew can be frozen for a week or two. After that, its spicy punch diminishes.

Superb Shrimp-and-Sausage Stew

Succulent shrimp, richly flavored beef sausage, and whole baby vegetables make this robust stew especially attractive. Serve with crunchy slaw and hearty rye crisp bread.

5- to 6-quart cooker   **Makes 6 servings.**

1 medium potato, cut into ¾-inch cubes

8 ounces baby carrots

1 can (15 ounces) baby corn, drained

1 large white onion, cut into thin wedges

½ cup fat-free chicken broth

1 can (16 ounces) low-sodium stewed tomatoes

1 bay leaf

1 teaspoon chili powder

1 clove garlic, minced

½ pound smoked sausage, cut in half lengthwise and sliced ½ inch thick

½ pound medium shrimp, shelled and deveined

Combine the potatoes, carrots, corn, onions, broth, tomatoes, bay leaf, chili powder, and garlic in an electric slow cooker.

Brown the sausage in a nonstick skillet over medium heat. Transfer to the slow cooker, and stir to combine. Cover and cook on LOW for 8 to 10 hours.

During the last hour of cooking, stir in the shrimp. Cover and cook until the shrimp are done, about 1 hour. Discard the bay leaf.

Per serving: About 414 calories, 9.2 g fat (19% of calories), 0.3 saturated fat, 57 mg cholesterol, 464 mg sodium, 7.6 g dietary fiber.

Cook's note: Be sure to add the shrimp during the last hour of cooking, not sooner.

Teriyaki Beef with Broccoli

This Asian-style dish is easy to make and fairly bursting with teriyaki's ginger-garlic flavor.

3½- to 4-quart cooker   **Makes 4 servings**

Nonstick spray

1 pound beef rump roast, cut into thin ¾- × 2-inch strips

4 carrots, cut into 2-inch-long sticks

1 package (20 ounces) frozen pearl onions

1 can (14 ounces) fat-free beef broth

2 tablespoons low-sodium teriyaki sauce

½ cup water

½ pound broccoli florets

8 ounces thin or medium noodles

Coat a nonstick skillet with garlic-flavored nonstick spray, and sauté the beef over medium-high until browned, about 5 minutes. Transfer the beef to an electric slow cooker.

Add the carrots, onions, broth, 1 tablespoon of teriyaki sauce, and water. Cover and cook on LOW until the meat is tender, 4 to 6 hours (or on HIGH, 7 to 9 hours). In the last half-hour, cook the noodles separately and drain them; keep warm.

Meanwhile, stir the broccoli into the beef mixture. Cover and cook until the broccoli is crisp-tender, about 5 minutes. Divide the noodles among 4 plates. Top with the beef mixture, and sprinkle with the remaining teriyaki.

Per serving: About 516 calories, 7.7 g fat (13% of calories), 2 g saturated fat, 60 mg cholesterol, 637 mg sodium, 6.1 g dietary fiber.

Cook's note: If reduced-fat canned broth isn't available, use the regular version and defat it. Here's what to do: Refrigerate the broth (unopened) for about 3 hours. The fat will rise to the top and congeal. Open the can and skim off the fat.

Thai-Spiced Pineapple and Pork Stew

For the world-traveler within, a taste of Thailand's sweet-spicy cuisine at its finest. The cooking method is slow-cooker easy, of course.

5- to 6-quart cooker   **Makes 6 servings**

1 pound boneless pork loin chops, cut into ¾-inch cubes

2 teaspoons canola oil

1 can (20 ounces) pineapple chunks in juice, drained, juice reserved

Juice of 1 lime

2 teaspoons low-sodium soy sauce

1 tablespoon honey

1 teaspoon Thai seasoning

4 cloves garlic, slivered

1 sweet red pepper, cut into thin strips

1 pound cherry tomatoes

1¼ cup medium-grain rice

1 lime, thinly sliced

Brown the pork on all sides in the oil in a nonstick skillet over medium-high heat. Transfer the pork to an electric slow cooker.

Combine the reserved pineapple juice, lime juice, soy sauce, honey, Thai seasoning, and garlic in a 4-cup measure. Add enough water to equal 2 cups. Mix well, and pour into the slow cooker.

Add the peppers and tomatoes. Cover and cook on HIGH for 3½ hours. Stir in the rice; add the lime slices. Cover and cook until the rice is tender and the liquid has been absorbed, about 1 hour.

Per serving: About 375 calories, 7 g fat (17% of calories), 1.9 g saturated fat, 40 mg cholesterol, 238 mg sodium, 1.6 g dietary fiber.

Cook's note: When adding the rice, stir the mixture gently so as not to split the tomatoes.

Winter Vegetable Stew with Cheddar and Croutons

A hearty, flavorful stew for healthy appetites. And it's vitamin A-okay, courtesy of the carrots and broccoli.

5- to 6-quart cooker   **Makes 4 servings**

1 potato, cut into ½-inch cubes

1 turnip, cut into ½-inch cubes

2 carrots, diagonally sliced ½ inch thick

1 celery stalk, diagonally sliced ½ inch thick

1 leek, white part only, sliced ½ inch thick

1 can (14 ounces) fat-free chicken broth

1 teaspoon dried savory

¼ teaspoon black pepper

¼ pound broccoli florets

3 cups **toasted croutons**

1 cup shredded Cheddar cheese

Bacon-flavored bits, for garnish

Combine the potatoes, turnips, carrots, celery, leek, broth, savory, and pepper in an electric slow cooker. Cover and cook on LOW until the vegetables are tender, 7 to 9 hours (or on HIGH for 4 to 6 hours).

Add the broccoli. Cover and cook until the broccoli is tender, about 15 minutes. Divide the stew among 4 bowls; top each serving with croutons, cheese, and bacon-flavored bits.

Per serving: About 320 calories, 11 g fat (30% of calories), 6.3 g saturated fat, 30 mg cholesterol, 604 mg sodium, 3.8 g dietary fiber.

Cook's note: To make **toasted croutons,** cut 3 slices of crusty bread into ½-inch cubes. Spread the cubes on a baking sheet or perforated pizza pan. Mist the cubes with nonstick spray, then broil them until they're golden, about 5 minutes. Shake or stir cubes to expose the uncooked sides; broil them until golden, about 3 minutes.

Marvelous Main Dishes

Popular convention has us prepare meals at the end of a long, hectic day. Well, that's about to change! Make these delicious entrées early in the day when you're rested and eager to cook: Black Bean and Corn-Stuffed Peppers, Herbed Italian Chicken, Paprika Chicken in Wine, Meat Loaf with Carrots and Onions, Spiced Turkey Breast with Pineapple, Pasta Shells and Sauce with Chick-Peas, and 27 others.

American Paella

Wild rice makes classic Spanish paella an American main course. Complete this delicious one-dish meal with a favorite dessert.

5- to 6-quart cooker   **Makes 6 servings**

2⅓ cups fat-free chicken broth

1½ cups coarsely chopped red onion

3 cloves garlic, finely chopped

½ pound boneless, skinless chicken breasts, cut into 1-inch cubes

1 jar (4 ounces) roasted peppers, drained

1 teaspoon turmeric

½ teaspoon dried thyme leaves

⅛ teaspoon black pepper

⅓ cup wild rice

1 cup long-grain brown rice

½ pound shrimp, shelled and deveined

1 cup frozen peas

Combine the broth, onions, garlic, chicken, roasted peppers, turmeric, thyme, and black pepper in an electric slow cooker. Cover and cook on HIGH for 3 to 5 hours.

Stir in the shrimp and wild and brown rices. Cover and cook until the shrimp and rices are tender and most of the liquid has been absorbed, about 1¼ to 2 hours. Add more water while the rice is cooking, if needed. Stir in the peas and cook until they're tender, about 15 minutes.

Per serving: About 349 calories, 3.8 g fat (10% of calories), 0.7 g saturated fat, 89 mg cholesterol, 190 mg sodium, 5.7 g dietary fiber.

Beef Kabobs with Vegetables

Kabobs with a tasty twist: No-fuss slow-cooking replaces watch-'em-close grilling. Serve with a spinach salad with a tomato viniagrette.

5- to 6-quart rectangular cooker (or an electric skillet)   **Makes 4 servings**

- 8 bamboo skewers
- Nonstick spray
- 1 pound rump roast, cut into 1-inch cubes
- 5 small potatoes, quartered
- 2 medium carrots, sliced ½ inch thick
- 2 medium onions, cut into wedges
- 1 can fat-free beef broth
- 1 tablespoon honey
- ¾ teaspoon ground cinnamon
- ¼ teaspoon black pepper
- ⅛ teaspoon ground allspice and ⅛ teaspoon ground cloves
- 2 tablespoons garlic-flavored vinegar
- 1 can (6 ounces) low-sodium tomato paste

Trim skewers to fit electric slow cooker. Coat a nonstick skillet with nonstick spray. Add meat and sauté it over medium-high heat until browned, about 6 minutes. Slide meat, potatoes, carrots, and onions onto skewers, alternating meat and vegetable pieces. Place in the bottom of a slow cooker.

In a bowl, combine the broth, honey, cinnamon, pepper, allspice, cloves, vinegar, and tomato paste. Mix well. Pour the broth mixture into the slow cooker and add enough water to barely cover the kabobs. Cover and cook on LOW until the vegetables are tender, 8 to 10 hours (on HIGH, 4 to 6 hours).

Per serving: About 338 calories, 5.6 g fat (15% of calories), 1.8 g saturated fat, 60 mg cholesterol, 156 mg sodium, 5.7 g dietary fiber.

Cook's note: No time for skewering meat and vegetables? That's okay. Simply skip that step and eliminate the added water. Voilà! A delicious, fast-to-fix stew.

Beef Roast with Mushroom-Onion Gravy

*Pot roast never tasted so good or was so easy to prepare. Serve with **Harvest Potatoes** (see page 98) and a green vegetable.*

5- to 6 quart cooker   **Makes 12 servings**

3 pounds bottom-round beef, trimmed of fat

3 medium onions, finely chopped

8 ounces mushrooms, thickly sliced

Butter-flavored nonstick spray

½ cup dry red wine

¼ teaspoon black pepper

¼ cup cold water

2 tablespoons cornstarch

1 teaspoon browning sauce

Brown the roast on all sides in a nonstick skillet over medium-high heat, 5 to 6 minutes; transfer to an electric slow cooker. In the skillet, sauté the onions until golden, about 3 minutes; transfer them to the slow cooker. Add the mushrooms to the same skillet, lightly coat with spray; sauté until golden, about 3 minutes. Transfer the mushrooms to the slow cooker.

Pour the wine into the slow cooker; sprinkle the roast with the pepper. Cover and cook on LOW until the roast is tender, 8 to 10 hours. Transfer the roast to a platter, leaving the onions, the mushrooms and liquid in the slow cooker. Keep the roast warm.

Combine the cold water, cornstarch and browning sauce in a measuring cup. Stir the cornstarch mixture into the onion-mushroom gravy, and cook, stirring often, until the gravy thickens, 2 to 3 minutes. Slice the roast; serve topped with gravy.

Per serving: About 245 calories, 8.5 g fat (32% of calories), 2.9 g saturated fat, 88 mg cholesterol, 95 mg sodium, 0.9 g dietary fiber.

Cook's note: The meat freezes well for up to a month. The gravy, once thickened with cornstarch, won't freeze well, but it'll keep in the refrigerator for a day or two.

Beef Rolls with Pickles

Savor the piquant flavors of beef, vegetables, and pickles in this updated German classic. And be sure to sop up its delicious gravy with mashed potatoes or hearty whole grain bread.

3½- to 4-quart cooker   **Makes 4 servings**

4 very thin round beef steaks (total, 1 pound)

1 teaspoon Dijon-style mustard

1 carrot, halved lengthwise and crosswise

1 onion, quartered

2 small dill pickles, halved

Kitchen string

½ cup fat-free beef broth

1 teaspoon browning sauce

1 tablespoon red wine vinegar

⅛ teaspoon black pepper

¼ cup cold water

2 tablespoons cornstarch

Pound the steaks to ⅛-inch thick; then spread ¼ teaspoon mustard on each. Place a carrot stick, onion quarter, and pickle half in the center of each steak. Roll up the steaks, and secure them with the string. Place the steak rolls in an electric slow cooker.

Combine the broth, browning sauce, vinegar, and black pepper in a measuring cup. Pour the broth mixture over the steak rolls in the slow cooker. Cover and cook on LOW for 6 to 8 hours or on HIGH for 4 to 6 hours. Transfer the beef rolls to a platter, leaving the liquid in the cooker. Keep the rolls warm. Combine the water and cornstarch in a measuring cup. Stir the cornstarch mixture into the gravy and cook, stirring often until the gravy thickens, 2 to 3 minutes. Serve the beef rolls topped with the gravy.

Per serving: About 209 calories, 6.8 g fat (30% of calories), 2.6 g saturated fat, 68 mg cholesterol, 533 mg sodium, 1.1 g dietary fiber.

Cook's note: Have metal skewers but no string? Use the skewers for securing the rolls. Carefully transfer the rolls to and from the slow cooker.

Black-Bean- and Corn-Stuffed Peppers

A delicious vegetarian dish that the whole family will love. It's packed with all the right stuff and makes a meal in itself.

3½- to 4-quart cooker   **Makes 4 servings**

½ cup rice, cooked

½ cup canned black beans, rinsed and drained

3 cloves garlic, minced

½ cup sliced scallions

½ cup frozen corn

2 plum tomatoes, diced

2 sprigs of cilantro, snipped

2 sprigs of parsley, snipped, or 2 teaspoons dried

3 fresh basil leaves, snipped, or ½ teaspoon dried

⅛ teaspoon white pepper

½ teaspoon chili powder

4 large sweet green peppers, with tops, membranes, and seeds removed

½ cup crushed tomatoes

½ cup water

2 ounces Monterey Jack or Cheddar cheese, shredded

Combine the rice, beans, garlic, scallions, corn, diced tomatoes, cilantro, parsley, basil, white pepper, and chili powder in a bowl. Toss to mix well. Divide the rice mixture into 4 portions, and spoon a portion into each of the sweet peppers.

Pour the tomatoes and water into an electric slow cooker; place the peppers, upright, in the cooker. Cover and cook on LOW for 4 to 6 hours. Transfer the peppers to serving plates, and top each with a generous spoonful of hot tomatoes and shredded cheese.

Per serving: About 203 calories, 4.9 g fat (21% of calories), 2.8 g saturated fat, 13 mg cholesterol, 166 mg sodium, 3.7 g dietary fiber.

Cook's note: You can stuff these peppers the night before, if you wish. Place them in your slow cooker's removable ceramic bowl, cover it, and refrigerate the entire thing until about 30 minutes before you're ready to start the slow cooker. Then remove the bowl from the refrigerator and let it sit on the counter. After 30 minutes, cook the peppers according to the recipe directions.

Mesquite Barbecue Beef on Rolls

Holy smokes! Here's a speedy hot sandwich with enough robust taste to satisfy the heartiest appetites.

3½- to 4-quart cooker   **Makes 8 servings**

1 pound extra-lean ground beef

2 medium onions, finely chopped

1 medium sweet green pepper, chopped

1 clove garlic, minced

1½ cup **Slow-Cooked Barbecue Sauce** (see page 107) or store-bought barbecue sauce

1 can (15 ounces) pinto beans, rinsed and drained

½ teaspoon mesquite or other liquid smoke

8 whole wheat Kaiser rolls

Cook the beef in a nonstick skillet over medium-high heat until brown and crumbly, 4 to 6 minutes. Using a slotted spoon, transfer the beef to an electric slow cooker. Pour off and discard the drippings.

In the same skillet, sauté the onions and green peppers until translucent, 3 to 5 minutes. Transfer to the slow cooker. Stir in the garlic, barbecue sauce, beans, and liquid smoke. Cover and cook on LOW for 7 to 10 hours. Serve in the rolls.

Per serving: About 366 calories, 12 g fat (30% calories), 4.2 g saturated fat, 38 mg cholesterol, 462 mg sodium, 3 g dietary fiber.

Cook's note: For even less fat, make this meaty dish with ground turkey breast.

Chicken Athenos

A delightful Greek-inspired dish that's infused with cinnamon and lemon and topped with feta cheese. Serve with a favorite taverna *salad.*

3½- to 4-quart cooker   **Makes 4 servings**

Juice of 1 lemon

2 cinnamon sticks

4 cloves garlic, minced

1 can (16 ounces) cut tomatoes with basil

1 bay leaf

⅛ teaspoon black pepper

¼ cup dry sherry

1 onion, chopped

1 pound boneless, skinless chicken breasts, trimmed of fat and
   cut into 4 pieces

1 teaspoon olive oil

¼ cup crumbled feta cheese

8 ounces broad noodles

Sprigs of fresh mint, for garnish

Combine the lemon juice, cinnamon, garlic, tomatoes, bay leaf, pepper, sherry, and onions in an electric slow cooker.

Brown the chicken on both sides in the oil in a nonstick skillet over medium-high heat, 2 to 4 minutes. Transfer the chicken to the slow cooker. Cover and cook on LOW for 8 to 10 hours. Discard the bay leaf. In the last half-hour, cook the noodles separately; drain and keep warm. Serve topped with chicken.

Per serving: About 374 calories, 8.4 g fat (20% of calories), 2.6 g saturated fat, 119 mg cholesterol, 610 mg sodium, 3.6 g dietary fiber.

Cook's note: Since the time of Greek mythology, mint has been a symbol of hospitality. For a flavor twist fit for the gods, garnish this dish with a few fresh mint sprigs.

Chicken with Oranges and Mushrooms

The fragrant essence of orange commands attention in this superior sweet-and-sour entrée. Enjoy it with simple side dishes such as radicchio salad and parsley potatoes.

3½- to 4-quart cooker   **Makes 4 servings**

¼ teaspoon white pepper

1½ teaspoons paprika

1 tablespoon flour

1 pound boneless, skinless chicken thighs

Butter-flavored nonstick spray

4 ounces mushrooms, sliced

¼ cup chopped onions

¼ cup sweet green pepper, chopped

½ cup orange juice

2 tablespoons dry sherry

1½ teaspoons brown sugar

1 small orange, sliced

Whisk together the flour, paprika, and pepper; sprinkle over both sides of the chicken pieces. Mist the pieces with the butter-flavored spray, and brown them in a nonstick skillet over medium-high heat, about 5 minutes. Transfer the chicken to an electric slow cooker.

Coat the same skillet with the nonstick spray, and sauté the mushrooms over medium-high heat until golden, 3 to 4 minutes. Transfer the mushrooms to the slow cooker. Add the onions and peppers.

In a measuring cup, mix the juice, sherry, and sugar. Pour over the chicken and vegetables. Top with the orange slices. Cover and cook on LOW until the chicken is tender and cooked through, 8 to 10 hours.

Per serving: About 334 calories, 13 g fat (35% of calories), 3.5 g saturated fat, 107 mg cholesterol, 190 mg sodium, 1.9 g dietary fiber.

Cook's note: For a meal with less fat and cholesterol, substitute chicken breasts for the thighs.

Chicken with Cider Vinegar Sauce

A simply delectable marriage of sweet and savory flavors. This elegant entrée–chicken breasts stuffed with spinach and apricots–takes about an hour to prepare.

3½- to 4-quart cooker   **Makes 4 servings**

- 1 teaspoon light margarine
- ⅔ cup chopped shallots
- 1 tablespoon sugar
- 1 tablespoon cider vinegar
- ½ cup fat-free chicken broth
- 1 pound boneless, skinless chicken breasts, trimmed of fat, cut into 4 pieces and pounded to ⅛ inch thick
- 8 ounces fresh spinach, stems removed
- 4 halves of canned apricots
- 1 tablespoon raisins
- 1 slice of sweet onion, quartered
- ¼ cup drained canned mandarin oranges
- Kitchen string
- Butter-flavored nonstick spray
- ¼ cup cold water
- 2 tablespoons cornstarch

Mix the margarine, shallots, sugar, vinegar, and broth in an electric slow cooker.

Place the chicken on a work surface, and top each piece with 5 or 6 spinach leaves. Divide the apricots, raisins, onions, and oranges evenly among the chicken pieces. Roll up the chicken, starting at a narrow end and enclosing the fruit-vegetable filling. Tie each roll with the string.

Coat a nonstick skillet with butter-flavored nonstick spray and warm over medium-high heat. Add the chicken rolls and brown them on all sides, 2 to 4 minutes. Transfer the rolls to the slow cooker. Cover and cook on LOW until the chicken is tender, 6 to 8 hours. Transfer the rolls to a platter, leaving the shallots and liquid in the slow cooker. Keep the rolls warm.

Combine the water and cornstarch in a measuring cup. Stir the cornstarch mixture into the vinegar sauce, and cook on HIGH, stirring frequently, until the sauce thickens, 1 to 2 minutes. Serve the sauce over the rolls.

Per serving: About 300 calories, 6 g fat (18% of calories), 1.4 g saturated fat, 96 mg cholesterol, 157 mg sodium, 2 g dietary fiber.

Cook's note: These rolls can also be made with turkey breast slices.

Turkey Slices with Favorite Fruit

Turkey gets a not-too-sweet apple-and-currant sauce in this recipe.

3½- to 4-quart cooker   **Makes 4 servings**

1 pound turkey breast slices

1 teaspoon olive oil

2 shallots, thinly sliced

½ cup dried apples or peaches

½ cup currants or golden raisins

⅛ teaspoon freshly ground black pepper

¼ cup water

Juice of 1 lemon

1 lemon thyme sprig or ¾ teaspoon dried thyme

2 lemons, thinly sliced

Brown the turkey on both sides in the oil in a nonstick skillet over medium-high heat, about 5 minutes. Transfer the turkey to an electric slow cooker. Add the shallots.

Mix the apples, currants, pepper, water, and juice in a small bowl. Pour the mixture over the turkey. Add the thyme and top with the lemon slices. Cover and cook on LOW until the turkey is done and the fruit is tender, 5 to 7 hours. Discard the thyme sprig.

Per serving: About 275 calories, 4.5 g fat (14% of calories), 0.7 g saturated fat, 95 mg cholesterol, 70 mg sodium, 2.3 g dietary fiber.

Chicken Stroganov

Named after Count Paul Stroganov, a 19th-century Russian diplomat, traditional stroganov is rich with butter, beef, and sour cream. This 20th-century version packs the same intriguing flavors but has far less fat and fewer calories.

3½- to 4-quart cooker   **Makes 4 servings**

1 pound boneless, skinless chicken breasts, cut into 1-inch cubes

4 teaspoons olive oil

2 medium onions, chopped

1½ cups mushrooms, sliced

½ cup dry white wine

¼ teaspoon black pepper

1 teaspoon paprika

½ cup nonfat sour cream

8 ounces broad egg noodles

Paprika, for garnish

In a skillet over medium-high heat, brown the chicken on all sides in 2 teaspoons of the oil, about 5 minutes. Transfer the chicken to an electric slow cooker.

In the same skillet over medium-high heat, sauté the onions and mushrooms in the remaining oil until the onions are golden, 3 to 4 minutes. Transfer the onion mixture to the slow cooker. Pour in the wine, and sprinkle the onion mixture with the pepper and paprika. Cover and cook on LOW until the chicken is tender and cooked through, 7 to 9 hours. In the last half-hour of cooking, cook and drain the noodles separately; keep them warm.

Using a slotted spoon, transfer the chicken to a platter, leaving the onion mixture and liquid in the slow cooker. Keep the chicken warm. Stir the sour cream into the onion mixture. Serve the chicken over the hot noodles, top with the sour cream sauce, and garnish with the paprika.

Per serving: About 507 calories, 9.7 g fat (18% of calories), 1.9 g saturated fat, 96 mg cholesterol, 107 mg sodium, 2.9 g dietary fiber.

Cook's note: To cut uncooked chicken breasts quickly and easily, use kitchen shears.

Chinese Chicken with Vegetables

Subtly seasoned with five-spice powder, this recipe captures the essence of a Shanghai-style dish.

3½- to 4-quart cooker **Makes 4 servings**

 2 strips bacon

 1 pound boneless, skinless chicken breast, cut into 1-inch pieces

 1 cup thinly sliced celery

 1 medium potato, cut into ¾-inch cubes

 1 cup sliced scallions

 1 can (8 ounces) bamboo shoots

 1½ teaspoons five-spice powder

 ¾ cup water

 1 tablespoon dry sherry

 1 tablespoon low-sodium soy sauce

 2 tablespoons cornstarch

 1 teaspoon sugar

Cook the bacon in a skillet over medium heat until crumbly, about 5 minutes. Drain on paper towels, crumble, and transfer to an electric slow cooker.

Pour off all but 2 teaspoons of the bacon drippings, and add the chicken to the skillet. Brown the chicken on all sides; then transfer it to the slow cooker. Stir in the celery, potatoes, scallions, bamboo shoots, five-spice powder, ½ cup of the water, and the sherry and soy sauce. Cover and cook on LOW until the chicken is cooked through and tender, 6 to 8 hours. In a measuring cup, combine the cornstarch, remaining water, and sugar. Pour into the chicken mixture and cook until the liquid has thickened, about 3 minutes.

Per serving: About 280 calories, 5.9 g fat (19% of calories), 1.8 g saturated fat, 99 mg cholesterol, 360 mg sodium, 1.9 g dietary fiber.

Cook's notes: Five-spice powder, a pungent blend of cinnamon, cloves, fennel seed, star anise, and szechuan peppercorns, is available in Asian markets and in most supermarkets. For added color, garnish with thin strips of sweet red pepper.

Curried Chicken over Rice

A blend of curry, cumin, turmeric, and ginger gives this dish its captivating Asian flavor and rich golden color. Serve with a side dish of steamed peas.

3½- to 4-quart cooker　　　　　　　　　　　　**Makes 4 servings**

　1 pound boneless, skinless chicken breasts, trimmed of fat and
　　　cut into 1-inch cubes

　4 medium onions, halved lengthwise and thinly sliced

　4 cloves garlic, minced

　1 tablespoon low-sodium soy sauce

　1 teaspoon curry powder

　2 teaspoons chili powder

　1 teaspoon turmeric

　1 teaspoon ginger powder

　1 tablespoon peanut oil

　⅓ cup water

　1⅛ cups rice

Mix the chicken, onions, garlic, soy sauce, curry, chili, turmeric, ginger, oil and water in an electric slow cooker. Cover and cook on LOW until the chicken is tender and cooked through, 7 to 9 hours. In the last half-hour, cook the rice separately; keep it warm. Serve the chicken over the hot rice.

Per serving: About 346 calories, 8 g fat (21% of calories), 1.8 g saturated fat, 96 mg cholesterol, 241 mg sodium, 2.6 g dietary fiber.

Cook's note: The cooked curried chicken mixture can be frozen for up to a month. To reheat it, thaw it in the refrigerator, then heat it until hot and bubbly throughout. Freeze the rice separately for up to two months, and thaw it in the refrigerator as well. Add one or two tablespoons of water to the rice before warming it.

Fajitas with Cumin Seeds

A lime-and-pepper marinade gives traditional steak fajitas their flavor and tenderness. Here, slow cooking achieves the same mouth-watering results.

3½- to 5-quart cooker   **Makes 4 fajitas**

¾ pound lean chip steak, cut into thin strips

¼ cup fat-free beef broth

2 medium onions, halved lengthwise and thinly sliced

1 medium sweet green or red pepper, thinly sliced

6 cloves garlic, minced

½ teaspoon cumin seeds

1 chili pepper, minced

½ cup frozen corn

½ cup cooked black beans

Juice of 1 lime

4 flour or corn tortillas (8-inch diameter)

4 tablespoons nonfat sour cream

½ cup medium or hot salsa

Sprigs of cilantro, for garnish

Combine the steak, broth, onions, sweet pepper, garlic, cumin, chili pepper, corn, and beans in an electric slow cooker. Cover and cook on LOW until the steak is tender, 7 to 9 hours. Stir in half the lime juice.

Divide the steak mixture among the tortillas; then roll them up. Place them in a microwave-safe baking dish and sprinkle them with the remaining lime juice. Warm everything in a microwave oven on high for 1 minute. To warm in a regular oven, cover with foil and place in a preheated oven for 5 minutes at 325°F (163°C). Top with the sour cream and salsa, and garnish with the cilantro.

Per fajita: About 377 calories, 9.3 g fat (22% of calories), 3.2 g saturated fat, 34 mg cholesterol, 378 mg sodium, 3 g dietary fiber.

Cook's note: Ground cumin is a perfectly acceptable replacement for cumin seeds. Use a little less, however.

Glazed Turkey Breast Roast

Not just for company: This tender, stuffed roast tastes as good as it looks! It's easy to prepare, too.

5- to 6-quart cooker   **Makes 6 servings**
(plus a collapsible vegetable steamer basket)

2 bay leaves

1 teaspoon assorted peppercorns

Water to fill one inch of cooker

Nonstick cooking spray

3 cups sourdough bread cubes

⅓ cup finely chopped Canadian bacon

1 medium onion, chopped

2 celery stalks, chopped

2 cloves garlic, minced

¼ cup fat-free chicken broth

¼ teaspoon white pepper

½ teaspoon sage

1½ pounds boneless turkey breast

½ cup currant, apricot or apple jelly

Place the bay leaves and peppercorns in an electric slow cooker. Add water to approximately 1 inch. Place a collapsible vegetable steamer basket in the slow cooker.

Coat a nonstick skillet with nonstick spray, and warm it over medium-high heat. Sauté the bread, bacon, onions, celery, and garlic until the onions are lightly browned, about 6 minutes. Stir in the white pepper and the sage. Transfer the bread stuffing to the steamer basket in the slow cooker.

Coat the same skillet with nonstick spray; rewarm over medium-high heat. Quickly brown the turkey breast on both sides; then transfer it to the slow cooker, placing it atop the stuffing.

Melt ¼ cup jelly and brush it on the turkey breast. Cover and cook on LOW until the breast is tender and cooked through, 190°F (87.8°C) on a meat thermometer, 8 to 10 hours. Melt the remaining jelly and brush it on the breast.

Per serving: About 310 calories, 3 g fat (9% of calories), 0.9 g saturated fat, 104 mg cholesterol, 406 mg sodium, 1.3 g dietary fiber.

Spiced Turkey Breast with Pineapple

The warm, intense flavors of cinnamon and cloves contrast with the sweet lusciousness of pineapple in this delightful dish. Serve with creamy mashed potatoes and steamed carrots and peas.

5- to 6-quart cooker   **Makes 4 servings**

¼ cup jellied cranberry sauce

1 tablespoon cider vinegar

¼ cup fat-free chicken broth

1 tablespoon brown sugar

¼ teaspoon ground cinnamon

⅛ teaspoon ground cloves

⅛ teaspoon white pepper

1 pound turkey tenders or turkey breast, cut into 4 strips

1 cup chopped onions

3 cloves garlic, minced

10 ounces canned pineapple chunks, drained

Combine the cranberries, vinegar, broth, brown sugar, cinnamon, cloves, and pepper in a measuring cup. Pour half of the cranberry mixture into an electric slow cooker. Add the tenders, and top them with the onions, garlic and pineapple. Pour the remaining cranberry mixture over everything. Cover and cook on LOW until the turkey is tender and cooked through, 6½ to 9 hours.

Per serving: About 251 calories, 1 g fat (4% of calories), 0.3 g saturated fat, 95 mg cholesterol, 89 mg sodium, 1.4 g dietary fiber.

Cook's note: Don't worry if the cranberry mixture is slightly lumpy; the jellied cranberries will dissolve when heated.

Herbed Italian Chicken

This Italian-inspired chicken-and-mushroom entrée rates A-1 for flavor and ease of preparation. It can also be the basis of Chicken Parmigiana. Serve it with mashed potatoes and a simple slaw salad.

3½- to 4-quart cooker   **Makes 4 servings**

½ cup dry white wine

1 tablespoon balsamic vinegar

1 pound boneless, skinless chicken breasts,
   cut into 4 pieces

2 teaspoons olive oil

4 cloves garlic, chopped

¼ teaspoon crushed red pepper flakes

1 teaspoon Italian herb seasoning

⅛ teaspoon white pepper

4 ounces white mushrooms, sliced,
   or 2 portobello mushrooms, diced

2 shallots, sliced

4 plum tomatoes, sliced

2 tablespoons seasoned dry bread crumbs

Snipped fresh parsley, for garnish

Pour the wine and vinegar into an electric slow cooker. In a skillet over medium-high heat, brown the chicken on all sides in 1 teaspoon of the oil, for about 5 minutes. Transfer the chicken to the slow cooker, and sprinkle each piece with the garlic and pepper flakes, herb seasoning, and white pepper.

In the same skillet, sauté the mushrooms in the remaining oil until golden, about 4 minutes. Spoon them over the chicken. Top everything with the shallots. Cover and cook on LOW until the chicken is tender, 7 to 9 hours.

Transfer the chicken and toppings to a broiler-safe pan; top the chicken with the tomatoes and the crumbs. Broil until the crumbs are golden, about 1 minute, and garnish with the parsley.

Per serving: About 279 calories, 5.7 g fat (19% of calories), 1.4 g saturated fat, 96 mg cholesterol, 119 mg sodium, 1.3 g dietary fiber.

Cook's note: For **Chicken Parmigiana,** grate 4 ounces of part skim milk mozzarella cheese and 2 ounces of Parmesan cheese. Top the chicken, tomato, and bread-crumb mixture with the shredded mozzarella and Parmesan cheeses. Broil until the cheese is melted and has just started to brown.

Heritage Pork Roast

A braised roast with mustard-sage seasoning and a side of apple-flavored sweet potatoes. Serve with a light spinach salad.

5- to 6-quart cooker　　　　　　　　　　　**Makes 6 servings**

½ cup apple juice or cider

1½ pounds sweet potatoes, peeled and sliced 1 inch thick

3 medium onions, sliced and separated into rings

4 medium apples, peeled and sliced

2 pound center-cut boneless pork roast, trimmed of fat

1 teaspoon Dijon mustard

¼ teaspoon black pepper

4 fresh sage leaves, snipped, or ⅛ teaspoon dried sage

¼ cup cold water

1 teaspoon brown sugar

2 tablespoons cornstarch

Pour the apple juice into an electric slow cooker. Then layer the sweet potatoes, onions, and apples in the slow cooker.

In a nonstick skillet, brown the pork on all sides over medium-high heat. Place the pork on top of the potato and apple slices. Brush the mustard over the roast and sprinkle the roast with the pepper and sage. Cover and cook on LOW until the roast is done and registers 165°F (73.9°C) on a quick reading meat thermometer, 7 to 9 hours.

Transfer the roast to a platter and keep it warm. Using a slotted spoon, transfer the apple–sweet potato mixture to a bowl and keep it warm.

Combine the water, sugar, and cornstarch in a measuring cup. Stir the cornstarch mixture into the juices in the cooker, and cook, stirring often, until they thicken, 1 to 2 minutes. Serve it over the apple-potato mixture and the roast.

Per serving: About 426 calories, 11.8 g fat (25% of calories), 3.5 g saturated fat, 88 mg cholesterol, 179 mg sodium, 4.4 g dietary fiber.

Cook's note: Don't be surprised if the apples seem to disappear during cooking; their wonderful, sweet flavor remains.

Lemon-Onion Pork Chops

The tangy flavor of lemon prevails in this delicious, fast-to-prepare dish. Serve with spinach salad topped with a fat-free blue cheese dressing or steamed French-cut green beans.

3½- to 4-quart cooker   **Makes 4 servings**

1 cup canned crushed tomatoes with basil

4 boneless ½-inch-thick center-cut loin pork chops, trimmed of fat

Freshly ground black pepper

1 lemon, cut into 4 slices

1 medium onion, cut into 4 slices

4 sprigs of fresh thyme or lemon thyme, or ½ teaspoon dried thyme

1 bay leaf

4 scrubbed potatoes, in their jackets

Spoon half the tomatoes into the electric slow cooker. Arrange the pork chops in a single layer over the tomatoes. Sprinkle with the pepper. Top each chop with a lemon slice and an onion slice. Add the thyme and bay leaf. Spoon the remaining tomatoes over the chops. Cover and cook on LOW until the pork is tender, 7 to 9 hours.

In the oven, bake the potatoes at 425°F (218°C) until done, about 1 hour, or microwave on HIGH, turning once, for 20 minutes. Discard the thyme and bay leaf. Serve the lemony tomato sauce over the chops and potatoes.

Per serving: About 325 calories, 7 g fat (20% of calories), 2.5 g saturated fat, 61 mg cholesterol, 224 mg sodium, 3.5 g dietary fiber.

Cook's notes: The chops and sauce can be frozen for up to a month. To reheat them, thaw them in the refrigerator, then heat them until the pork is hot and the sauce is hot and bubbly throughout. Potatoes develop a mealy texture when frozen, so cook fresh potatoes right before serving.

Meat Loaf with Carrots and Onions

Remember Mom's delicious, home-style meat loaf? It's here. Prepare it early in the day so it is ready to eat when you are.

5- to 6-quart cooker with steaming rack   **Makes 8 servings**

1 cup finely chopped tomatoes

4 sprigs of fresh parsley, finely chopped, or ¼ cup dried

3 egg whites, beaten

¼ teaspoon freshly ground black pepper

1 medium onion, shredded

1 dried cayenne pepper, minced, or ½ teaspoon crushed red pepper flakes

2 cups dry bread crumbs

½ cup ketchup

6 fresh sage leaves, snipped, or 1 teaspoon dried sage

2 medium carrots, finely shredded

½ cup corn

1 tablespoon red wine vinegar

1 pound extra-lean ground round

1 cup fat-free beef broth

1 cup water

Combine the tomatoes, parsley, egg whites, black pepper, onions, cayenne pepper, bread crumbs, ¼ cup ketchup, sage, carrots, corn, and vinegar in a large bowl. Add the ground beef and mix thoroughly.

Place a steaming rack or metal vegetable steaming basket in an electric slow cooker. Pour the broth and water into the cooker. Shape the beef mixture into an oblong or round loaf, depending on the slow cooker's shape, and place the loaf on the rack. Cover and cook on HIGH until the meat is done, 4 to 6 hours. Brush the remaining ketchup over the meat loaf. Cover and cook 15 minutes.

Per serving: About 310 calories, 12 g fat (34% of calories), 4.2 g saturated fat, 38 mg cholesterol, 386 mg sodium, 3.1 g dietary fiber.

Paprika Chicken in Wine

Whole spices and plenty of paprika impart a pleasantly intense flavor to this entrée. Serve with creamy mashed potatoes and a tomato and lettuce salad.

5- to 6-quart cooker   **Makes 4 servings**

½ cup dry white wine

2 teaspoons olive oil

1 pound boneless, skinless chicken breasts, trimmed of fat and cut into 4 pieces

1 teaspoon cumin seeds

1 teaspoon mustard seeds

4 cloves garlic, minced

1 tablespoon paprika

1 large onion, thinly sliced

4 ounces mushrooms, sliced

Sprigs of parsley, for garnish

Sweet red pepper rings, for garnish

Pour the wine into an electric slow cooker. Heat 1 teaspoon of the oil in a skillet, and brown the chicken on both sides over medium-high heat, 3 to 5 minutes. Transfer the chicken to the slow cooker, and sprinkle on the cumin, mustard, garlic, and paprika.

Add the remaining oil to the same skillet and sauté the onions and mushrooms until lightly browned, 2 to 3 minutes. Spoon over the chicken in the slow cooker. Cover and cook on LOW until the chicken is tender, 7 to 9 hours. Garnish with the parsley and peppers.

Per serving: About 268 calories, 7 g fat (24% of calories), 1.5 g saturated fat, 96 mg cholesterol, 89 mg sodium, 1.3 g dietary fiber.

Cook's note: To cook this dish in a 3½- to 4-quart slow cooker, cut the chicken into smaller pieces and put the seasonings between the layers.

Paprika Veal with White Beans

A boldly seasoned paste of garlic and paprika flavors this tender veal sirloin. Enjoy it with the accompanying mild-flavored, fiber-rich beans and strips of sweet red pepper.

5- to 6-quart cooker   **Makes 4 servings**

½ cup dry white wine

1 pound veal sirloin

2 tablespoons balsamic vinegar

4 cloves garlic, pressed

2 teaspoons paprika

2 leeks, white part only, sliced

1 sweet red pepper, sliced

2 slices crisp-cooked bacon, crumbled

1 can (14 ounces) great northern beans, rinsed and drained

Fresh basil leaves, for garnish

Pour the wine into an electric slow cooker. Add the veal.

In a measuring cup, combine the vinegar, garlic, and paprika. Using a pastry brush, paint the veal with the vinegar-garlic mixture. Top the veal with the leeks, peppers, and bacon. Place the beans in the wine around the veal. Cover and cook on LOW until the veal is cooked through, 8 to 10 hours.

Per serving: About 436 calories, 9 g fat (19% of calories), 3.4 g saturated fat, 121 mg cholesterol, 169 mg sodium, 6.3 g dietary fiber.

Cook's note: Rinsing canned beans helps reduce the sodium level.

Pecan-Rice Cabbage Packets

A symphony of fruity, nutty flavor simmers in these fast-to-fix bundles, each of which makes a complete meal. If currants and pecans aren't readily available, substitute raisins and walnuts.

5- to 6-quart cooker   **Makes 4 servings**

1 medium onion, chopped

¼ cup long-grain white or brown rice

¼ cup snipped fresh parsley

¼ cup finely chopped pecans

¼ cup currants

1 can (6 ounces) tomato paste

½ teaspoon sugar

¼ teaspoon ground allspice

¼ teaspoon paprika

4 large green cabbage leaves

1 cup fat-free chicken broth

1 cup water

Kitchen string

Mix together the onions, rice, parsley, pecans, currants, tomato paste, sugar, allspice, and paprika for the filling. Remove the tough rib from each cabbage leaf. Divide the filling among the leaves, placing some in the center of each. Fold in the leaf edges, and fasten each packet together with the string. Place the packets in an electric slow cooker.

Combine the chicken broth and water; pour it over the cabbage packets. Cover and cook on HIGH for 4 to 6 hours.

Per serving: About 195 calories, 5.7 g fat (25% of calories), 0.5 g saturated fat, 0 mg cholesterol, 126 mg sodium, 4.1 g dietary fiber.

Cook's note: To make tightly rolled packets, first blanch the cabbage leaves for 3 to 5 minutes and cool them; then add the filling. Finish cooking as per the recipe.

Pork Chops New Orleans

As in traditional Creole cooking, this palate-pleasing main course favors tomatoes, sweet peppers, and onions. Serve with slaw or steamed green beans or broccoli.

3½- to 4-quart cooker   **Makes 4 servings**

1 can (16 ounces) stewed tomatoes

Juice of 1 lemon

1 teaspoon Worcestershire sauce

Dash of Louisiana hot-pepper sauce

¼ cup dry white wine

Nonstick spray

1 medium onion, thinly sliced

1 sweet green pepper, thinly sliced

2 cloves garlic, minced

4 boneless center-cut loin pork chops, trimmed of fat and cut ½-inch thick

Dash of white pepper

¼ cup cold water

2 tablespoons cornstarch

1 cup rice

Combine the tomatoes, lemon juice, Worcestershire sauce, hot-pepper sauce, and wine in an electric slow cooker.

Coat a nonstick skillet with the nonstick spray, and sauté the onions, green peppers, and garlic over medium-high heat until the onions are golden, 3 to 5 minutes. Transfer the onion mixture to the slow cooker and mix well.

In the same skillet, brown the pork on both sides over medium-high heat. Place the pork on top of the tomato-onion mixture. Sprinkle the pork with the white pepper. Cover and cook on LOW until the pork is tender, 8 to 10 hours. In the last half-hour, cook the rice separately; keep warm. Transfer the pork to a platter, leaving the tomato-onion mixture in the slow cooker. Keep the pork warm.

Combine the water and cornstarch in a measuring cup. Stir the cornstarch mixture into the tomato-onion mixture, and cook on LOW, stirring often, until the liquid thickens, 1 to 2 minutes. Divide the rice among four serving plates; top it with the tomato-onion mixture and a pork chop.

Per serving: About 436 calories, 13.4 g fat (28% of calories), 4.6 g saturated fat, 81 mg cholesterol, 98 mg sodium, 1.3 g dietary fiber.

Cook's note: What's the difference between Louisiana hot sauce and tabasco? Plenty of heat–that's what! Of the two, Louisiana is the milder. If you choose to use tabasco, measure it in drops, not teaspoonsful.

Quick Beef-and-Lentil Tacos

The heat's up, but not too much. These Tex-Mex tacos are boldly seasoned with chili, yet remain palate cool 'n' friendly. Serve with crisp vegetable crudités, such as carrots, sweet peppers, cauliflower, and broccoli.

3½- to 4-quart cooker   **Makes 16 tacos**

1 pound extra-lean ground beef

2 medium onions, chopped

½ sweet green pepper, chopped

1 carrot, finely shredded

4 cloves garlic, minced

1⅓ cups crushed tomatoes

1⅓ cups dry lentils

1 cup water

1 tablespoon chili powder

1 teaspoon ground cumin

16 soft flour taco shells or flour tortillas

1 or 2 jalapeño peppers, minced (optional)

For garnish

1 cup shredded Monterey Jack cheese

Torn lettuce

1 large tomato, chopped

Medium-hot or hot salsa

Brown the beef in a large nonstick skillet over medium-high heat, 5 to 7 minutes. Using a slotted spoon, transfer the beef to an electric slow cooker. With paper towels, wipe most of the fat from the skillet, then add the onions and green pepper. Cook until the onions are translucent, about 5 minutes.

Transfer the onion mixture to the slow cooker. Stir in the carrots, garlic, tomatoes, lentils, water, chili powder, and cumin. Cover and cook on LOW until the lentils are tender, 6 to 8 hours.

Spoon the beef-lentil mixture into the taco shells, and fold the shells in half. Place the filled shells on a baking sheet, and cover them with foil. Warm in a 325°F (163°C) oven for 5 minutes. Garnish each taco with the cheese, lettuce, tomatoes, and salsa.

Per taco: About 254 calories, 7.6 g fat, (27% of calories), 2.3 g saturated fat, 19 mg cholesterol, 241 mg sodium, 0.8 gm. dietary fiber.

Cook's notes: For fiery hot tacos, add one or two minced jalapeño peppers during the last hour of cooking.

You can refrigerate the beef-lentil mixture for up to 3 days. When you are ready to serve it, heat it until hot throughout, then spoon it into the shells. Warm the shells; then garnish as in the recipe.

Picadillo de Pavo

Translated, this means turkey hash. *Here, warm flour tortillas enclose a zesty combination of turkey, tomatoes, raisins, and seasonings for a family-pleasing, south-of-the-border-style dish.*

3½- to 4-quart cooker   **Makes 4 servings**

Nonstick spray

1 pound ground turkey breast

1 large red onion, chopped

4 cloves garlic, minced

1 pound plum tomatoes, thinly sliced

1 large green chili, chopped

1 teaspoon chili powder

1 teaspoon ground allspice

½ cup raisins

8 flour tortillas

8 green stuffed olives, sliced, for garnish

Medium or hot salsa (optional)

Nonfat sour cream (optional)

Coat a nonstick skillet with the nonstick spray. Cook the turkey in the skillet over medium-high heat, stirring frequently, until the meat is browned and crumbly, 4 to 5 minutes. Add the onions and garlic, and cook until the onions are translucent, 3 to 4 minutes. Transfer the mixture to an electric slow cooker.

Stir in the tomatoes, chili pepper, chili powder, allspice, and raisins. Cover and cook on LOW for 5 to 7 hours.

Divide the turkey mixture among the tortillas; garnish with the olive slices; serve with the optional salsa and sour cream.

Per serving: About 491 calories, 6.7 g fat (12% of calories), 1.1 g saturated fat, 95 mg cholesterol, 584 mg sodium, 2.9 g dietary fiber.

Cook's note: Corn tortillas make a tasty substitute for the wheat flour ones, and picante sauce can replace the salsa.

Red- and Black-Bean Chili

Perfect for fall and winter suppers, this spicy dish packs plenty of healthful fiber. Serve with carrot and celery crudités and crusty sourdough bread.

5- to 6-quart cooker   **Makes 8 servings**

1 pound extra lean ground beef

6 cloves garlic, minced

3 large onions, chopped

2 large sweet green peppers, chopped

2 chili peppers, minced

1 can (28 ounces) crushed tomatoes

1 cup water

4 cups home-cooked red kidney beans, or 2 cans (15 ounces each), rinsed and drained

2 cups home-cooked black beans, or 1 can (16 ounces), rinsed and drained

3 tablespoons chili powder

1 teaspoon ground cumin

¼ teaspoon ground allspice

¼ teaspoon ground coriander

1 tablespoon red wine vinegar or cider vinegar

Brown the beef in a nonstick skillet over medium-high heat, until the meat is browned and crumbly, about 3 minutes. Spoon off the fat as it accumulates. Add the garlic and onions, and cook until the onions are translucent, about 3 minutes.

Transfer the beef mixture to an electric slow cooker. Add the sweet peppers and chili peppers, tomatoes, water, red and black beans, chili powder, cumin, allspice, coriander, and vinegar. Cover and cook on LOW for 6 to 8 hours.

Per serving: About 353 calories, 8 g fat (20% of calories), 2.9 g saturated fat, 45 mg cholesterol, 243 mg sodium, 8.7 g dietary fiber.

Cook's note: This hearty chili tastes superb the second day. Store it in the refrigerator, and reheat it until hot and bubbly.

Savory Turkey Meatballs in Italian Sauce

Seasoned just right with garlic, onion, and cheese, these meatballs have the taste of those grandmom used to make, but only a fraction of the fat. Enjoy them with spaghetti or in a hoagie roll.

5½- to 6-cup cooker **Makes 8 servings**

1 can (28 ounces) crushed tomatoes

1 tablespoon red wine vinegar

1 medium onion, finely chopped

2 cloves garlic, minced

¼ teaspoon Italian herb seasoning

1 teaspoon dried basil

1 pound ground turkey breast

2 egg whites

⅛ teaspoon garlic powder

¼ teaspoon dried minced onion

⅛ teaspoon black pepper

⅓ cup quick oats

⅓ cup dried parsley

¼ cup grated Parmesan cheese

¼ cup unbleached flour

Nonstick spray

Combine the tomatoes, vinegar, onions, garlic, seasoning, and basil in an electric slow cooker. Cover and turn slow cooker on to LOW. In a bowl, mix the turkey, egg whites, garlic powder, dried onions, pepper, oats, parsley, and cheese. Form into 16 one-inch balls, and dredge each ball in the flour. Lightly mist the balls with the nonstick spray and brown them on all sides in a nonstick skillet over medium-high heat. Transfer them to the slow cooker. Cover and cook on LOW for 8 to 10 hours.

Per serving: About 183 calories, 2.2 g fat (11% of calories), 0.9 g saturated fat, 50 mg cholesterol, 349 mg sodium, 2.8 g dietary fiber.

Cook's notes: These keep nicely in the freezer for up to a month.

Pasta Shells and Sauce with Chick-Peas

Saucy but simple, this version of traditional Italian pasta and beans goes together in minutes. Enjoy it with a crisp salad and a glass of red wine.

3½ to 4-quart cooker   **Makes 6 servings**

1 can (28 ounces) crushed tomatoes

1 can (19 ounces) chick-peas, rinsed and drained

6 cloves garlic, minced

1 teaspoon sugar

1 teaspoon Italian herb seasoning

1 tablespoon red wine vinegar

4 slices dried eggplant, finely chopped (optional)

6 fresh basil leaves, finely snipped

12 ounces medium pasta shells

2 tablespoons grated Parmesan cheese

Combine the tomatoes, chick-peas, garlic, sugar, seasoning, vinegar, and eggplant (if you wish to use eggplant) in an electric slow cooker. Cover and cook on LOW for 6 to 8 hours to make the sauce. During the last hour, cook the shells separately and drain them; keep warm. Stir the basil into the sauce and serve it over the pasta. Top each serving with the cheese.

Per serving: About 444 calories, 3.8 g fat (8% of calories), 0.5 g saturated fat, 1.6 mg cholesterol, 382 mg sodium, 2.2 g dietary fiber.

Sweet and Sour Beef

Honey and vinegar, vegetables, and fruit provide the wonderfully complex flavors in this one-dish dinner. Bonus: Fiber's high; calories and fat are low.

3½- to 4-quart cooker   **Makes 4 servings**

Nonstick spray

½ pound rump roast, cut into 1-inch cubes

1 orange, sections cut into 1-inch cubes

1 cup dried apricot halves

2 small onions, cut into thin wedges

1 cup chopped sweet green pepper

1 cup fat-free beef broth

2 tablespoons apple cider vinegar

2 tablespoons low-sodium soy sauce

1 tablespoon honey

⅛ teaspoon ground red pepper

2 teaspoons arrowroot starch

2 tablespoons cold water

8 ounces medium egg noodles

Coat a nonstick skillet with nonstick spray. Add the meat and sauté it over medium-high heat until browned, about 5 minutes. Transfer it to an electric slow cooker. Add the apricots, onions, and green peppers.

Stir in the broth, vinegar, soy sauce, honey, and red pepper. Cover and cook on LOW for 6 to 7 hours or on HIGH for 3½ to 5 hours. During the last half-hour, make the egg noodles separately and drain; keep them warm.

Dissolve the arrowroot in the cold water. Stir the arrowroot mixture into the broth mixture in the cooker, and cook until the sauce is slightly thickened, about 4 minutes. Serve over the hot noodles.

Per serving: About 441 calories, 3.7 g fat (7% of calories), 1.0 g saturated fat, 30 mg cholesterol, 364 mg sodium, 5.1 g dietary fiber.

Cook's note: Can't find any arrowroot? Thicken the sauce with cornstarch instead.

Turkey Cutlets and Pasta with Black Olives

Cheese, olives and turkey form a tasty trio in this easy-to-make entrée. Serve with a mixed green salad or hot steamed peas.

3½- to 4-quart cooker   **Makes 4 servings**

1 pound turkey cutlets, cut into 1- × 3-inch pieces

1 teaspoon olive oil

1 medium onion, finely chopped

¼ cup canned chopped roasted sweet peppers

4 cloves garlic, minced

½ cup fat-free chicken broth

2 tablespoons dry sherry

½ teaspoon Louisiana hot sauce

¼ teaspoon dried thyme leaves

¼ cup evaporated skim milk

¼ cup grated Parmesan cheese

8 ounces ziti or rotini

8 black olives, sliced

Brown the turkey in the oil in a skillet over medium-high heat, 3 to 5 minutes. Transfer to an electric slow cooker. Add the onions, peppers, garlic, broth, sherry, hot sauce, and thyme. Cover and cook on LOW until the turkey is cooked through and tender, 6 to 8 hours. In the last half-hour, cook the pasta separately; drain and keep warm.

Meanwhile, stir the milk and cheese into the turkey mixture. Cook until the mixture is hot, 15 to 30 minutes. Serve it over the pasta and top with the olives.

Per serving: About 503 calories, 6.6 g fat (12% of calories), 1.9 g saturated fat, 100 mg cholesterol, 387 mg sodium, 3.9 g dietary fiber.

Cook's note: Low-fat (1%) milk may be substituted for the evaporated skim milk.

Veal Cutlet Roulade

In this dish, Swiss chard and shallots are wrapped in tender lean meat. The result: an entrée that's elegant enough for a sophisticated dinner, easy enough for every-night fare.

5- to 6-quart cooker   **Makes 4 servings**

1 pound veal cutlets, pounded to ¼ inch thick

4 Swiss chard leaves, stems removed

2 shallots, thinly sliced

½ teaspoon dried savory leaves

Kitchen string

Olive-flavored nonstick spray

½ cup uncooked barley

½ cup fat-free chicken broth

½ cup water

1 tablespoon white wine vinegar

⅛ teaspoon white pepper

Freshly ground black pepper, for garnish

Snipped fresh chives, for garnish

Place the veal on a work surface. Top each cutlet with some chard and shallots. Sprinkle with the savory. Roll up each cutlet; tie it closed with a piece of kitchen string.

Coat a nonstick skillet with the nonstick spray, and brown the veal roll on all sides over medium-high heat.

Combine the barley, broth, water, and vinegar in an electric slow cooker. Transfer the veal to the slow cooker; sprinkle with the white pepper. Cover and cook on LOW until the veal is tender, 7 to 9 hours.

Serve the veal with the barley; garnish the barley with the black pepper and chives.

Per serving: About 285 calories, 6.4 g fat (20% of calories), 1.7 g saturated fat, 99 mg cholesterol, 152 mg sodium, 3.6 g dietary fiber.

Cook's note: For variety, substitute spinach for the Swiss chard and small onions for the shallots.

Sensational
Accompaniments

Sauces and side dishes: What would plain pasta and roasted meats be like without them? Here are 17 no-hassle accompaniments—including All-Day Simmered Spaghetti Sauce, New-Fashioned Baked Beans, and Zin Cranberries—that add flavor and pizzazz to main courses.

Acorn Squash with Pepper-Rice Stuffing

This quick-and-easy vegetarian dish is long on flavor, short on fat.

5- to 6-quart rectangular cooker   **Makes 4 side dish servings**

1 acorn squash (about 1½ pounds)

¼ cup long-grain rice

1 carrot, coarsely shredded

1 small sweet green pepper, chopped

2 cloves garlic, minced

1 teaspoon turmeric

½ cup water

½ cup vegetable broth

¼ cup nonfat sour cream, for garnish

¼ cup snipped fresh parsley, for garnish

Cut the squash in half lengthwise and remove the seeds. Combine the rice, carrots, peppers, garlic and turmeric, and spoon the mixture into the squash cavities.

Pour the water into an electric slow cooker, and add the squash halves, cavity-sides up. Pour the broth into the rice mixture in each cavity. Cook on LOW until the squash and rice are tender, 5 to 7 hours. Serve garnished with the sour cream and parsley.

Per serving: About 136 calories, 0.4 g fat (2% of calories), 0.1 g saturated fat, 0 mg cholesterol, 34 mg sodium, 3.3 g dietary fiber.

Cook's note: To serve this as a main dish, top each helping with shredded Cheddar cheese or chopped nuts, and allow ½ squash per serving. (To cook 2 small squashes at once, use an electric skillet set to simmer, instead of a slow cooker.)

Balsamic Beets

Beet buffs take note: These burgundy-colored roots have a natural affinity for chervil butter and horseradish mustard.

5- to 6-quart cooker   **Makes 6 servings**

6 medium beets (about ½ pound each), peeled, with roots and
    tops removed

3 cups water (or enough to cover the beets in the cooker)

1 tablespoon balsamic vinegar

1 bay leaf

for Chervil Butter:

¼ cup butter, melted

2 teaspoons dried chervil

for Horseradish Mustard:

2 tablespoons horseradish

2 tablespoons Dijon mustard

Place the beets in an electric slow cooker. Add water, vinegar, bay leaf. Cover and cook on LOW until the beets are tender, 6 to 8 hours. Discard the bay leaf. Drain and slice beets; serve with the chervil butter or horseradish mustard.

Per serving: About 102 calories, 0.3 g fat (3% of calories), 0.1 g saturated fat, 0 mg cholesterol, 167 mg sodium, 7 g dietary fiber.

Cook's notes: To ensure even color, turn the beets once or twice during cooking. To make **chervil butter,** combine the melted butter and the dried chervil. To make **horseradish mustard,** mix the horseradish with the Dijon mustard.

Basic Wheat Dumplings

Complement your next stew with these quick-to-make steamed breads.

5- to 6-quart cooker   **Makes 8 dumplings**

⅔ cup unbleached flour

⅔ cup whole wheat flour

2 teaspoons baking powder

⅔ cup skim milk

2 tablespoons canola oil

Whisk the unbleached and whole wheat flours and baking powder together in a bowl.

In another bowl, mix the milk and the oil. Pour the liquid mixture into the flour mixture; stir with a fork until the ingredients are just combined.

Switch the heat to HIGH on an electric slow cooker filled with steaming stew. Drop 8 spoonfuls of dough in a single layer onto the stew. Cover and steam the dumplings until a toothpick inserted into the center of one comes out clean, about 30 minutes. To serve, top each dumpling with a generous serving of stew.

Per dumpling: About 112 calories, 3.8 g fat (30% of calories), 0.3 g saturated fat, 0 mg cholesterol, 15 mg sodium, 1.2 g dietary fiber.

Cook's note: For white dumplings, replace the whole wheat flour with unbleached flour.

Curried Butternut Squash with Cilantro

The distinctive and intriguing flavor of curry dominates in this fast-to-fix side dish. Serve with roast chicken or turkey.

3½- to 4-quart cooker   **Makes 4 servings**

¼ cup fat-free chicken broth

2 medium butternut squash, peeled and cut into 1-inch cubes

1 tablespoon curry powder

⅛ teaspoon freshly ground black pepper

4 sprigs of fresh cilantro, snipped

Pour the broth into an electric slow cooker. Toss the squash with the curry, and add it to the slow cooker. Cover and cook on LOW until the squash is tender, 6 to 8 hours. Transfer to a serving bowl and sprinkle with the pepper and cilantro.

Per serving: About 88 calories, 0.4 g fat (4% of calories), 0 g saturated fat, 0 mg cholesterol, 30 mg sodium, 4 g dietary fiber.

Cook's note: After 6 to 8 hours of cooking, the squash is very tender. For firmer squash, cook 4 to 5 hours.

Harvest Potatoes

Garlic and pickling spices give everyday potatoes a mellow, captivating flavor. Serve these taters with beef, pork, or lamb roasts.

3½- to 4-quart cooker   **Makes 8 servings**

1 cup fat-free chicken broth

2 teaspoons pickling spice, tied in cheesecloth

4 large potatoes, peeled and cut into ¾-inch cubes

2 cloves garlic, pressed

Snipped fresh chives, for garnish

Pour the broth into an electric slow cooker, and place the spices in the center bottom of the cooker. Add the potatoes and garlic. Cover and cook on LOW for 5 to 6 hours. Garnish with the chives.

Per serving: About 69 calories, 0.3 g fat (4% of calories), 0 g saturated fat, 0 g cholesterol, 46 mg sodium, 1 g dietary fiber.

Cook's notes: These potatoes are best when served fresh. To make 4 servings, use small to medium potatoes. If pickling spice isn't available, substitute a bay leaf and a teaspoon each of whole peppercorns and whole nutmeg. These may be placed in a mesh tea ball for cooking.

Herbed Potatoes and Carrots

The natural sweetness of carrots pairs perfectly with the tart flavor of lemon. This easy recipe uses the herb lemon thyme.

3½- to 4-quart cooker   **Makes 4 servings**

2 carrots, cut into ½-inch slices

    2 medium potatoes, cut into ½-inch cubes

    4 large scallions, white part only, cut into ½-inch slices

    ¼ cup vegetable broth

    Dash of freshly ground black pepper

    Sprig of lemon thyme or ¼ teaspoon dried thyme leaves

Place the carrots, potatoes, and scallions in an electric slow cooker. Add the broth, pepper, and thyme. Cover and cook on HIGH until the vegetables are tender, 4 to 6 hours. Discard the lemon thyme.

Per serving: About 61 calories, 0.1 g fat (2% of calories), 0 g saturated fat, 0 mg cholesterol, 22 mg sodium, 1.9 g dietary fiber.

Maple-Candied Sweet Potatoes

Raisins and maple syrup bring out the natural sweetness of these golden potatoes. Serve them often; they're a snap to fix.

3½- to 4-quart cooker   **Makes 4 servings**

    ¼ cup maple syrup

    ¼ cup apple juice

    1 tablespoon butter

    4 small sweet potatoes, peeled

    ½ cup raisins

Mix the syrup and juice in an electric slow cooker. Add the butter, potatoes, and raisins. Cover and cook on LOW until the potatoes are tender, 8 to 10 hours. Serve with the syrup from the cooker and raisins spooned over the potatoes.

Per serving: About 253 calories, 3.1 g fat (11% of calories), 1.9 g saturated fat, 8 mg cholesterol, 45 mg sodium, 4.2 g dietary fiber.

New-Fashioned Baked Beans

This incredibly easy and great-tasting recipe makes enough for a small crowd. Why not simmer up a potful for your next potluck supper?

3½- to 4 quart cooker   **Makes 10 servings**

3 cups crushed tomatoes

2 cans (15 ounces each) great northern beans

½ pound Canadian bacon, cut into ¼-inch cubes

1 medium onion, minced

¼ cup brown sugar

1 tablespoon coarse brown mustard

2 tablespoons red wine vinegar

½ teaspoon hickory smoke flavoring

Combine the tomatoes, beans, bacon, onions, sugar, mustard, vinegar, and smoke flavoring in an electric slow cooker. Cover and cook on LOW for 7 to 9 hours.

Per serving: About 202 calories, 2.2 g fat (10% of calories), 0.7 g saturated fat, 11 mg cholesterol, 427 mg sodium, 5.2 g dietary fiber.

Cook's note: These spicy-sweet beans keep in the refrigerator for 3 to 4 days. Small white beans or white kidney beans can substituted for the great northerns.

Picante Lentil Sauce

Lentils and cumin impart complex earthy flavors to this south-of-the-border-style sauce. Enjoy it over omelets, burritos, spaghetti squash, pasta, or rice.

3½- to 4-quart slow cooker　　　　　　**Yields about 4 cups**

1 can (28 ounces) crushed tomatoes

¼ cup lentils, rinsed

2 medium onions, chopped

5 cloves garlic, minced

1 teaspoon sugar

½ teaspoon cumin seeds

1 fresh green chili, minced

½ cup medium-hot picante sauce

Combine the tomatoes, lentils, onions, garlic, sugar, cumin, chili, and picante sauce in an electric slow cooker. Cover and cook on LOW until the lentils are tender, 6 to 8 hours.

Per cup: About 158 calories, 0.8 g fat (4% of calories), 0 g saturated fat, 0 mg cholesterol, 532 mg sodium, 4.9 g dietary fiber.

Cook's note: The sauce can be cooked on LOW for up to 10 hours.

Pierogies in Pepper-Shallot Sauce

Here a chunky, robust sauce enhances the less intense flavors of potato-filled pierogies.

5- to 6-quart cooker   **Makes 6 servings**

1 can (28 ounces) crushed tomatoes

1 shallot, thinly sliced

1 cup chopped sweet green peppers

½ teaspoon olive oil

½ tablespoon red wine vinegar

½ teaspoon Italian herb seasoning

½ teaspoon black pepper

1 pound potato-filled pierogies, fresh or frozen

Combine the tomatoes, shallots, peppers, oil, vinegar, seasoning, and black pepper in an electric slow cooker. Cover and cook on LOW for 5 to 9 hours or on HIGH for 3½ to 5 hours. Add the pierogies. Cover and cook for 1 hour.

Per serving: About 179 calories, 2.1 g fat (10% of calories), 0.7 g saturated fat, 10 mg cholesterol, 522 mg sodium, 4.2 g dietary fiber.

Cook's note: Pierogies are Polish filled dumplings. Thaw frozen pierogies before adding them to the sauce.

Rosemary's Saucy Green Beans

Believe it or not, these beans are crisp-tender even after simmering for hours. And their flavor? It's the greatest!

3½- to 4-quart cooker   **Makes 8 servings**

1 pound fresh green beans

1 can (28 ounces) crushed tomatoes

2 strips crisp bacon, crumbled

4 cloves garlic, minced

1 teaspoon dried rosemary

⅛ teaspoon freshly ground black pepper

Combine the beans, tomatoes, bacon, garlic, rosemary, and pepper in an electric slow cooker. Cover and cook on LOW until the beans are tender, 5 to 7 hours.

Per serving: About 64 calories, 1 g fat (13% of calories), 0.3 g saturated fat, 1.3 mg cholesterol, 271 mg sodium, 2.7 g dietary fiber.

Cook's note: Though their flavor's not as intense, 2 tablespoons of store-bought bacon-flavored bits or 2 slices of minced Canadian bacon can replace the crumbled bacon.

Savory Turnip Bowls with Bacon and Onions

Here's a clever turnip presentation that's company-special yet everyday easy.

4-, 5- or 6-quart rectangular cooker　　　　　**Makes 2 servings**

¾ cup low-sodium vegetable broth

2 large white turnips, (12 ounces each), scrubbed

1 medium potato, quartered

1 small onion, quartered

1 tablespoon snipped fresh dill or 1 teaspoon dried dillweed

2 slices crisp bacon, crumbled

⅛ teaspoon freshly ground black pepper

Pour the broth into an electric slow cooker. Slice a thin piece from the bottom of each turnip so the turnips sit flat. Using a melon baller, scoop out the interior of each turnip, leaving a ¼-inch shell and reserving the interior. Place the shells in the slow cooker.

Shred the reserved turnip, potatoes, and onions in a food processor. Mix in the dill and bacon. Spoon the turnip mixture into the shells. Cover and cook on LOW until the turnip is tender, 3 to 5 hours. Sprinkle with the pepper.

Per serving: About 169 calories, 3.5 g fat (17% of calories), 1.2 g saturated fat, 5 mg cholesterol, 300 mg sodium, 1.6 g dietary fiber.

Cook's note: To cook 4 or more turnip bowls at once, use an electric skillet. Set the heat to simmer.

Simmered Spaghetti Sauce

Slow simmering blends the flavors in this superb chunky sauce. Serve it over your favorite pasta and enjoy it with warmed, crusty Italian bread and a tossed salad topped with red-wine vinaigrette.

3½- to 4-quart cooker   **Yields about 6 cups**

1 teaspoon olive oil

1 can (6 ounces) low-sodium tomato paste

1 can (28 ounces) Italian plum tomatoes

3 medium onions, finely chopped

4 cloves garlic, minced

1 celery stalk, finely chopped

¾ cup water

¼ teaspoon black pepper

¼ teaspoon chili powder

¼ teaspoon ground allspice

1 tablespoon sugar

¼ teaspoon dried thyme leaves

1 bay leaf

⅓ cup snipped fresh parsley, or 1 tablespoon dried

⅓ cup snipped fresh basil, or 1 tablespoon dried

Mix the oil, tomato paste, tomatoes, onions, garlic, celery, and water in an electric slow cooker. Stir in the pepper, chili powder, allspice, sugar, thyme, and bay leaf. Cook on LOW for 8 to 10 hours. Discard the bay leaf. Stir in the parsley and basil during the last half-hour of cooking. Serve over your favorite spaghetti.

Per ½ cup: About 113 calories, 0.6 g fat (5% of calories), 0.1 g saturated fat, 0 mg cholesterol, 157 mg sodium, 1.9 g dietary fiber.

Cook's note: For a meat sauce, brown ¾ pound of extra lean ground meat, and add it to the slow cooker for all-day cooking.

Spaghetti Squash Steamed with Peppercorns

Slowly simmer spaghetti squash until it's al dente, and make one of the sauces in this book to go with it.

5- to 6-quart rectangular cooker   **Makes 4 servings**

2 cups water

1 tablespoon assorted peppercorns

1 spaghetti squash (3 pounds)

Picante Lentil Sauce or **Simmered Spaghetti Sauce**

Grated Parmesan cheese for topping

Place the water and peppercorns in an electric slow cooker. Using a sturdy two-pronged fork or a paring knife, pierce the shell of the squash in numerous places so it doesn't explode. Place it in the slow cooker. Cover and cook on LOW until the squash is tender, 7 to 9 hours. Serve topped with sauce and grated Parmesan cheese.

Per serving: About 31 calories, 0.1 g fat (3% of calories), 0.1 g saturated fat, 0 mg cholesterol, 5 mg sodium, 2.2 g dietary fiber.

Slow-Cooked Barbecue Sauce

A basic sauce with a tomato-onion flavor and just a hint of sweetness. It's great for jazzing up grilled meats and poultry. Feel free to use it liberally; it's low in fat and sodium.

3½- to 4-quart cooker   **Yields about 2½ cups**

1 can (15 ounces) crushed tomatoes

½ cup water

1 medium onion, chopped

¼ teaspoon chili powder

¼ teaspoon paprika

2 tablespoons sugar or brown sugar

1 tablespoon Dijon mustard

1 teaspoon Worcestershire sauce

2 tablespoons cider vinegar or red wine vinegar

Mix the tomatoes, water, onions, chili, paprika, sugar, mustard, Worcestershire, and vinegar in an electric slow cooker. Cover and cook on LOW for 4 to 6 hours.

Per ¼ cup: About 32 calories, 0.1 g fat (3% of calories), 0 g saturated fat, 0 mg cholesterol, 148 mg sodium, 1 g dietary fiber.

Cook's note: The sauce will keep in the refrigerator for up to a week.

Stuffed Pasta Shells with Mushroom Sauce

Store-bought shells minimize preparation time. The hearty sauce is rich with mushroom flavor.

5- to 6-quart cooker   **Makes 6 servings**

8 ounces mushrooms, sliced

2 teaspoons olive oil

2 soy-sausage breakfast patties

1 can (28 ounces) plum tomatoes, cut up

1 can (6 ounces) low-sodium tomato paste

½ teaspoon dried oregano

½ teaspoon garlic powder

½ cup dry white wine

1 package (20 ounces) low-fat cheese-stuffed pasta shells

Snipped fresh Italian parsley, for garnish

Sauté the mushrooms in the oil in a nonstick skillet until golden, about 5 minutes. Transfer them to an electric slow cooker.

In the same skillet, cook the sausage patties for 6 minutes. Remove them from the skillet, and cut them into ¼-inch cubes. Place the pieces in the slow cooker.

Stir in the tomatoes, tomato paste, oregano, garlic, and wine. Cover and cook on HIGH for 3½ to 5 hours.

Add the shells to the sauce, making certain to cover them with sauce. Cover and cook until the shells are thoroughly hot, about 1 hour. Garnish with the parsley.

Per serving: About 212 calories, 6.9 g fat (28% of calories), 1.9 g saturated fat, 8.3 mg cholesterol, 584 mg sodium, 3.4 g dietary fiber.

Cook's note: For a quick buffet dish, double the recipe and use either the stuffed shells or ravioli.

Stuffed Zucchini

Gardeners take note: Here's yet another tasty way to use the summer's bounty. Medium-sized produce make the best squash boats.

4- to 6-quart rectangular cooker　　　　　**Makes 4 servings**

1 medium zucchini, halved lengthwise, with seeds removed

1 cup low-sodium tomato sauce

1 tablespoon red wine vinegar

1 small onion, finely chopped

2 cloves garlic, chopped

¼ cup brown rice

¼ cup snipped fresh parsley

4 basil leaves, snipped

⅛ teaspoon black pepper

2 tablespoons toasted pine nuts, for garnish

Place the zucchini in the bottom of an electric slow cooker. In a measuring cup, combine the tomato sauce and vinegar.

In a bowl, combine the onions, garlic, rice, parsley, basil, pepper, and 2 tablespoons of the tomato sauce mixture. Spoon the rice mixture into the zucchini "boats." Top with the remaining tomato mixture. Cover and cook on LOW until the rice is tender, 4 to 6 hours. Garnish with the pine nuts.

Per serving: 89 calories, 0.5 g fat (5% of calories), 0.1 g saturated fat, 0 mg cholesterol, 22 mg sodium, 2 g dietary fiber.

Cook's note: To toast pine nuts (also called pignolias or piñons), place them in a small nonstick skillet. Then warm them over medium heat, shaking the skillet occasionally, until they're golden, about 5 minutes.

Zin Cranberries

Fruity and sweet, zin cranberries garner rave reviews from holiday dinner guests. Serve with turkey and pork roasts.

5- to 6-quart cooker   **Yields about 7 cups**

2 packages (12 ounces each) fresh cranberries

3 cups sugar

2 cups California Zinfandel wine

1 cinnamon stick

2 teaspoons grated orange peel

2 oranges, segments cut into ¾-inch pieces

¾ cup currants

Mix the cranberries, sugar, Zinfandel, cinnamon, orange peel, and orange segments in an electric slow cooker. Cover and cook on HIGH until at least half of the cranberries pop, 5 to 7 hours. Remove the cinnamon stick, and stir in the currants. Cool to room temperature, then chill.

Per ½ cup: About 245 calories, 0.2 g fat (1% of calories), 0 g saturated fat, 0 mg cholesterol, 24 mg sodium, 2.9 g dietary fiber.

Cook's note: Refrigerated in a covered container, the cranberries will keep for up to 3 weeks.

Sweet Endings

Walnut-Raisin Apple Bake, Heavenly Poached Pears, Light Swedish Rice Pudding, Hot Chocolate. These and other yummy, home-style treats have gotten a fuss-free, fast-to-fix makeover. Now they're as tasty as ever, but so quick to make that you can put them back on the menu every day. Enjoy!

Almond-Ginger-Peach Puree

An uncommonly rich sauce that's marvelous by itself or as a topping for angel food cake or frozen vanilla yogurt. For crunch, top the whole thing with a sprinkling of no-fat-added granola.

3½- to 4-quart cooker　　　　　**Makes 16 servings (¼ cup each)**

2 cups (7 ounces) dried peach halves

1 cup dried apple slices

3 cups white grape juice

3 tablespoons sugar

2 tablespoons brown sugar

2 teaspoons minced crystallized ginger

1 cinnamon stick

½ teaspoon almond extract

Combine the peaches, apples, grape juice, sugars, ginger, and cinnamon in an electric slow cooker. Cover and cook on LOW until the peaches are very tender, 6 to 8 hours (on HIGH, 3½ to 5 hours). Discard the cinnamon and stir in the almond.

Per ¼ cup: About 110 calories, 0.2 g fat (1% of calories), 0 g saturated fat, 0 mg cholesterol, 9 mg sodium, 2.3 g dietary fiber.

Cook's note: The sauce stores beautifully in the refrigerator for several days. To serve warm, heat briefly (5 to 15 seconds) in a microwave set on MEDIUM.

Bread Pudding with Raisins and Walnuts

Custardy and rich-tasting, this dessert is a fresh version of the treat my mother used to make with "day-old" bread.

3½- to 4-quart cooker   **Makes 8 servings**

1 egg

3 egg whites

2 cups packed soft white bread cubes

3 cups skim milk

1 teaspoon light margarine

⅔ cup sugar

½ teaspoon vanilla

½ cup coarsely broken walnuts

½ cup raisins

Nonfat whipped topping, for garnish

Beat the egg and egg whites together in a large bowl. Mix in the bread, milk, margarine, sugar, vanilla, walnuts, and raisins. Pour the mixture into an electric slow cooker. Cover and cook on LOW until a knife inserted into the center of the pudding comes out clean, 2½ to 3½ hours. Serve warm or chilled, and garnish with the nonfat whipped topping.

Per serving: About 219 calories, 5.9 g fat (23% of calories), 0.7 g saturated fat, 28 mg cholesterol, 137 mg sodium, 1 g dietary fiber.

Cook's note: For more fiber, replace the white bread with whole wheat bread. You can keep this special treat in the refrigerator for up to 3 days.

Cinnamon-Spiced Apple Cider

Cider and spice and everything nice! That's what this warming beverage is made of. Enjoy it for the holidays, during quiet times by the fire—anytime a soothing drink is in order.

3½- to 4-quart cooker   **Makes 16 servings (½ cup each)**

3 Macintosh apples, peeled and thinly sliced

2 quarts apple cider or juice

2 cinnamon sticks

6 whole cloves

Whipped cream (optional)

Nutmeg (optional)

Place the apples in an electric slow cooker. Add the cider and the cinnamon. Cover and cook on LOW until the cider is hot and the apples are tender, about 4 hours. Serve mugfuls with slices of apple. Top with a dollop of cream and a pinch of nutmeg, if you wish.

Per serving: About 75 calories, 0.2 g fat (3% of calories), 0 g saturated fat, 0 mg cholesterol, 4 mg sodium, 0.5 g dietary fiber.

Cook's note: Serve with spoons so people can eat the apples.

Cranberry-Orange Pear Slices

A scrumptious, chunky sauce for topping nonfat cakes and ice creams.
Hostesses, note: This sauce is easily doubled, even tripled, to serve a crowd.

5- to 6-quart cooker   **Makes 6 servings**

1½ cups jellied cranberry sauce

¼ cup orange juice

1 teaspoon orange peel

4 slightly underripe pears, peeled and sliced

3 cups nonfat vanilla ice cream

Place sauce, juice, peel, and pears in an electric slow cooker. Cover and cook until the pears are tender, 6 to 8 hours. Serve warm over the ice cream.

Per serving: About 278 calories, 0.5 g fat (2% of calories), 0 g saturated fat, 0 mg cholesterol, 74 mg sodium, 3.9 g dietary fiber.

Cook's note: To make a pear puree, use fully ripe pears. After cooking, use a hand-held blender to puree the pears.

Heavenly Poached Pears

*Topped with luscious **almond cream**, these spicy pears make a grand finale worthy of the fanciest dinner party, but are easy to make.*

5- to 6-quart cooker   **Makes 8 servings**

Juice of 1 lemon

1 cup water

8 slightly underripe Bartlett, Anjou, or Bosc pears, peeled

2 tablespoons crystallized ginger

2 teaspoons lemon peel

2 tablespoons white sugar

5 tablespoons brown sugar

1 teaspoon ground cinnamon

2 cups white grape juice

for the Almond Cream:

1 cup plain low-fat yogurt

1 cup nonfat sour cream

½ teaspoon almond extract

Place the lemon juice and water in a medium bowl; dip the pears into the lemon mixture to keep them from browning. Stand the pears up in an electric slow cooker.

Combine the ginger, 1 teaspoon of lemon peel, white sugar, 2 tablespoons of brown sugar, cinnamon, and grape juice in a measuring cup; pour the juice mixture over the pears. Cover and cook on LOW until the pears are tender, about 5 hours. Remove the pears from the heat and let them cool in the poaching liquid.

To Make the Almond Cream: While the pears are cooking, drain the yogurt in a cheesecloth-lined strainer in the refrigerator. When ready to serve the pears, combine the drained yogurt (yogurt cheese), sour cream, remaining brown sugar, and almond extract; stir until well blended. Serve each pear with a dollop of almond cream; garnish with the remaining peel.

Per serving: About 212 calories, 0.7 g fat (3% of calories), 0 g saturated fat, 1 mg cholesterol, 42 mg sodium, 4.7 g dietary fiber.

Hot Chocolate

On a brisk day, enjoy a warm-you-up treat that's always a family favorite.

3½- to 4-quart cooker   **Makes 5 servings (6 ounces each)**

4 cups skim or low-fat (1%) milk

¼ cup sugar

⅓ cup chocolate-flavored syrup

Marshmallows, marshmallow creme, or nonfat whipped topping

Mix the milk, sugar, and syrup in an electric slow cooker. Cover and cook on LOW until the milk is hot, 2 to 3 hours. Stir, and ladle into mugs. Garnish with the marshmallows, marshmallow creme or whipped topping.

Per serving: About 131 calories, 0.5 g fat (3% of calories), 0.3 g saturated fat, 2.9 mg cholesterol, 94 mg sodium, 0 g dietary fiber.

Cook's note: If you're in a hurry for hot milk, heat it on HIGH for an hour; then turn the slow cooker to LOW. Left on HIGH, the milk might scorch.

Hot Cranberry Punch

Cranberry flavor and color prevail in this spicy, not-too-sweet refresher. Ladle it hot into mugs garnished with lemon slices. Ummm! It's delightful.

3½- to 4-quart cooker   **Makes 16 servings (½ cup each)**

1 quart apple juice

1 quart cranberry juice

6 whole cloves

4 lemon herbal tea bags

1 cinnamon stick

Lemon slices, for garnish

Pour the juices into an electric slow cooker. Add the cloves, tea, and cinnamon. Cover and cook on LOW until hot, about 3 hours.

Remove the cinnamon and tea bags. Ladle into mugs, and garnish each serving with a lemon slice.

Per serving: About 60 calories, 0.1 g fat (2% of calories), 0 g saturated fat, 0 mg cholesterol, 3 mg sodium, 0.1 g dietary fiber.

Cook's note: Substitute orange tea and slices for the lemon, if desired.

Peach and Apple Compote

An after-dinner winner, this compote, which has nary a gram of fat, will surely satisfy your sweet tooth. It's great for breakfast and snacks, too.

3½- to 4-quart cooker   **Makes 8 servings**

1 cup dried peach halves

1 cup dried apple slices

½ cup golden raisins

½ cup currants

1 cup dried apricot halves

1 cinnamon stick

2¾ cups water

Juice of 1 lemon

1 teaspoon grated lemon peel

1 tablespoon brown sugar

Frozen nonfat vanilla ice cream or yogurt (optional)

Combine the peaches, apples, raisins, currants, apricots, and cinnamon in an electric slow cooker. Stir in the water, lemon juice and peel, and sugar. Cover and cook on LOW until the fruit is tender, 5 to 7 hours. Discard the cinnamon stick. Serve with ice cream or yogurt, if you wish.

Per serving: About 150 calories, 0.2 g fat (1% of calories), 0 g saturated fat, 0 mg cholesterol, 13 mg sodium, 3.4 g dietary fiber.

Cook's notes: Stir the cooked fruit gently. The compote keeps, covered, in the refrigerator for several days.

Pumpkin Pudding

An old-fashioned custardy pudding that'll evoke fond memories of holiday desserts. The best part: It's nutritious and delicious.

3½- to 4-quart cooker   **Makes 8 servings**

1 egg

2 egg whites

1¾ cup canned or home-cooked pureed pumpkin

2 cans (12 ounces each) evaporated skim milk

1 teaspoon light margarine

⅓ cup brown sugar

⅓ cup white sugar

1 teaspoon ground cinnamon

½ teaspoon ground allspice

½ teaspoon ground nutmeg

½ cup raisins or chopped dates

2 cups packed soft bread cubes

1½ cups brandied yogurt topping

for Brandied Yogurt Topping:

2 cups low-fat vanilla yogurt

Cheesecloth

1 teaspoon brandy extract

Beat the egg and egg whites together until they're a light lemon color. Combine the eggs, pumpkin, milk, and margarine in an electric slow cooker. Stir in the sugars, cinnamon, allspice, nutmeg, raisins or dates, and bread cubes. Cover and cook on LOW until a knife inserted in the center of the pudding comes out clean, 5½ to 7½ hours.

Per serving: About 232 calories, 1.5 g fat (6% of calories), 0.5 g saturated fat, 30 mg cholesterol, 206 mg sodium, 2.1 g dietary fiber.

Cook's note: To make **brandied yogurt topping,** place 2 cups low-fat vanilla yogurt in a cheesecloth-lined strainer or colander. Let it drain in the refrigerator while the pudding is cooking. Stir 1 teaspoon brandy extract into the drained yogurt.

Light Swedish Rice Pudding

This no-fuss, cardamom-spiced dessert is comfort food at its very best.

3½- to 4-quart cooker   **Makes 6 servings**

4 cups skim milk

¼ cup medium-grain rice

½ cup sugar

½ teaspoon ground cardamom

½ teaspoon vanilla

¾ cup vanilla nonfat yogurt

Cinnamon-sugar, for garnish

Mix the milk, rice, sugar, and cardamom in an electric slow cooker. Cover and cook on LOW until the rice is very soft, 7 to 8 hours. Remove the rice from the cooker, and stir in the vanilla. Let cool at room temperature for about 1 hour; stir in the yogurt. Chill until cold, at least 4 hours. Garnish each serving with the cinnamon-sugar.

Per serving: About 156 calories, 0.3 g fat (2% of calories), 0.2 g saturated fat, 2.7 mg cholesterol, 102 mg sodium, 0 g dietary fiber.

Cook's note: To increase the fiber in this old-fashioned pudding, replace the white rice with brown rice, and add ½ cup of raisins when you remove the bowl from the heat.

Walnut-Raisin-Apple Bake

Looking for a carefree, applicious dessert? This sweet treat will fill the bill. Serve it with your favorite nonfat frozen topping.

4-, 5- or 6-quart rectangular cooker   **Makes 4 apples**

½ cup apple cider

Juice of 1 lemon

2 teaspoons maple syrup

2 tablespoons raisins

1 tablespoon dark brown sugar

1 teaspoon ground cinnamon

1 teaspoon ground walnuts

4 large Macintosh apples, cored

Pour the cider, lemon juice, and maple syrup into an electric slow cooker.

Combine the raisins, sugar, cinnamon, and walnuts in a small bowl. Place the apples in the slow cooker. Using a spoon, fill the center of the apples with the raisin mixture. Cover and cook on LOW until the apples are tender, 2 to 3 hours.

Per apple: About 140 calories, 1.3 g fat (7% of calories), 0.1 g saturated fat, 0 mg cholesterol, 4.0 mg sodium, 3.4 g dietary fiber.

Cook's note: Like firm baked apples? Replace the Macintosh apples with Golden Delicious.

Unit Conversions and Metric Equivalents

U. S. Liquid Measure Conversions

1 cup = 8 fluid ounces

1 cup = 16 tablespoons

1 cup = 48 teaspoons

1 cup = 236 mL (milliliters)

4.2 cups = 1 L (liter)

1 fluid ounce = 29.5 mL

1 fluid ounce= 6 teaspoons

1 fluid ounce = 2 tablespoons

1 tablespoon = ½ fluid ounce

1 tablespoon = 3 teaspoons

1 tablespoon = 15 mL

1 teaspoon = ⅙ fluid ounce

1 teaspoon = 5 mL

U. S. Mass (Weight) Conversions

1 ounce = ¹/₁₆ pound

1 ounce = 28.35 g (gram)

1 ounce = .028 kg (kilogram)

British Liquid Measure Conversions

1 Imperial cup = 10 Imperial fluid ounces

1 Imperial cup = 284 mL

1 Imperial fluid ounce = 28.4 mL

Index